Practical
problem

UXBRIDGE COLLEGE LEARNING CENTRE
Park Road, Uxbridge, Middlesex UB8 1NQ
Telephone: 01895 853326

Please return this item to the Learning Centre on
or before the last date stamped below:

HALE, R. et al.   658.403
Practical Problem Solving and Decision
making

Practical problem solving & decision making

An Integrated Approach

Richard Hale & Dr. Peter Whitlam

**KOGAN
PAGE**

To Eric and Elen Whitlam, with love.

YOURS TO HAVE AND TO HOLD

BUT NOT TO COPY

First published in 1997

Kogan Page Limited
120 Pentonville Road
London N1 9JN

© Richard I Hale and Peter J Whitlam, 1997

British Library Cataloguing in Publication Data

A CIP record for this book is available from the British Library.

ISBN 0 7494 2219 X

Typeset by JS Typesetting, Wellingborough, Northants
Printed in England by Clays Ltd, St Ives plc

CONTENTS

INTRODUCTION

Arguably one of the most fundamental of life skills required by human beings is the ability to solve problems and make decisions. Effectively it is this unique behaviour that has contributed significantly to the successful evolution of mankind and has been instrumental in determining our success as a species.

In today's society the skills of problem solving are just as, if not more, important than they were in the days of our ancestors. In fact it has been suggested by many futurists that one of the major societal changes we will experience is an increase in choice. Such choice may relate to factors such as how we do things, what we do and who we involve. Yet for most of us the process of problem solving is often viewed as intuitive — something that happens without explanation or undue thought, something that is shrouded in a kind of mystery. More recently though it has been possible to identify the mental stages through which an individual passes when engaged in problem solving and decision making and therefore to identify a powerful model for structured application in the organisational setting and beyond.

It is interesting to note that such cognitive processes appear to be the same irrespective of the nature or type of the problem being solved. As a consequence we have developed our own approach to the process of problem solving and devised a model which we believe mirrors in a more formal and structured way the mental stages through which individuals pass.

In addition we believe that as the world becomes a more turbulent and less predictable place, the requirement to solve complex problems increases dramatically. In the past, in a business context, many traditional approaches to solving problems and making decisions appear to have been somewhat random and *ad hoc*. In this book though we suggest that it is increasingly important to be able to demonstrate to others that a clear, systematic and logical process has been adopted in the process of problem solving, particularly when making recommendations for action. It is believed that this has become more important as we are frequently having to influence others regarding courses of action without necessarily being able to rely on position power or traditional hierarchical sources of authority. Furthermore individuals are becoming more demanding and questioning. No longer is it that easy to tell others what to do and expect them to follow slavishly. They are more likely to question one's thinking, rationale and logic and this means that the need to demonstrate that a systematic approach has been taken is increased.

Practical Problem Solving and Decision Making provides the reader with an opportunity to consider the skills of problem solving and decision making as part of an integrated and systematic process. In effect we are suggesting that if we follow certain clearly defined stages in the process of problem solving then we are much more likely to reach a satisfactory result or conclusion.

Although through the use of our Analysis, Decision Making, Active Risk Taking, Planning and Transition (ADAPT) model we recommend a specific approach which is valuable when dealing with more strategically oriented problems or project management related challenges, we also recognise that the model is not intended as a straitjacket; individual techniques can be used independently and are just as valuable when applied in stand-alone mode.

In writing the book we have placed the emphasis on it being written as a practical, no-nonsense guide aimed at simplifying the subject in a user-friendly manner. Our style is to commence each chapter with a brief overview of the objectives for the chapter and to conclude with a link to the subsequent stage in the process.

In some chapters we use *Case Studies* to illustrate specific points. Reference is made to the way in which we have used this unique approach to problem solving and decision making both in our own business and in working with organisations. We have used this approach in organisations such as Esselte, Motorola, Sheraton/ITT and Nestlé over the course of many years.

In addition we use the *Pause for Thought* sections at the end of the chapters as an approach which is intended to prompt readers to consider specific aspects of their own personal development and to relate the subject of the chapter to their own circumstances.

A unique feature of the book is the way in which we describe the ADAPT model of problem solving and decision making. This model provides a unique way of combining different techniques as well as enabling the individual to use specific techniques in a more flexible way.

WHO SHOULD READ THIS BOOK?

This book is suitable for any individual manager who wishes to improve his or her approach to problem solving and decision making. It has a particular relevance for complex or strategic problem solving or alternatively where there is a significant need to plan the management and implementation of change.

If read by a group or team the book provides a basis for understanding ways of improving collective problem solving and teamwork skills. Equally, the practical yet systematic style which has been adopted will ensure that it will also have a broad appeal to any manager who may have responsibility for project management.

STRUCTURE AND CONTENT

After an initial introduction, the structure of the book will follow the process of the ADAPT model as developed through our work with major international organisations. This model is an adaptation of the work of many individual contributors; the uniqueness is gained by the approach of pulling all these tools and techniques together in a cohesive and coherent whole.

Chapter I — The Nature of Problems

A primary aim of this initial chapter is to provide the reader with a rationale for reading the book, as well as offering an overview of the macro factors which are driving the case for a systematic approach to problem solving and decision making. A number of social and organisational trends are identified and it is shown how these form a driving force behind the move towards using groups and teams, often cross-functional, to solve problems.

The common reasons for the failure of projects are identified and it is shown how most, if not all, of these can be tackled through the implementation of the Analysis, Decision Making, Active Risk Taking, Planning and Transition (ADAPT) model.

The nature of problems is then explored and a categorisation of problems as either open or closed is suggested. Some examples of open and closed problems are provided and it is suggested that different analytical techniques should be used dependent on the nature of the problem.

We then go on to review the current state of the business planning process, and conclude that the classic business school model of business planning provides a useful framework for problem solving either at an organisational level or at a more local or project management level. It is argued that the use of a 'vision statement' is a prerequisite for a successful strategic approach to solving problems and various myths about the development and application of such statements are dispelled.

We show how the very act of producing a vision statement can help to unite a group; this should be underpinned with clarity of thought regarding the group's values and beliefs. We provide a framework for developing a vision statement and demonstrate a simple yet effective approach to evaluating the final output. We also consider the consequences of the existence of a clash between individual and organisational or team values and beliefs.

Chapter 2 — Exploring the Barriers

In this chapter the reader is introduced to the notion that effective problem solving and decision making is often about successfully managing the barriers which exist. Examples of common barriers to problem solving are identified; these include the following:

▓ Not knowing where to start
▓ Failure to understand perspectives
▓ Inappropriate techniques and process
▓ Need for a solution
▓ Perceptual distortions.

We make recommendations as to how these barriers can be managed including the use of techniques and tools such as the Problem Specification, the Seven Ms and using a Perspective Specification.

Chapter 3 — The ADAPT Model of Problem Solving

In this chapter we expand on the reader's understanding of the ADAPT model of problem solving and identify that in order to solve problems successfully, an individual needs to manage carefully a number of key steps, incorporating:

▓ Analysis
▓ Developing decisions
▓ Active risk management
▓ Planning and control.

The book then moves on to examine the key steps in the ADAPT model in more detail.

Chapter 4 — Approaches to Analysis

This chapter commences by exploring the concept of analysis and it is suggested that at the most basic level this is concerned with looking at the problem in more detail and in effect identifying further subsidiary problems as a result of the analysis.

This chapter then moves on to consider the use of two specific analytical techniques which are especially relevant in tackling open problems:

▓ Strengths, Weaknesses, Opportunities, Threats (SWOT) analysis
▓ Force Field Analysis.

Worked examples of these techniques are shown, drawing on our own experience in addressing real business problems. It is suggested that these two techniques are useful for exploring the 'big picture' in understanding a problem but also recognises that it may be necessary to follow up these with other techniques which provide a more detailed understanding of the problem.

At this point we discuss the use of closed techniques:

▓ The Why, Why Analysis
▓ The Fishbone Analysis.

Again, worked examples are used based on real business issues. The analysis stage is probably the most important stage in the process and the one which is most often overlooked.

Chapter 5 — The Dynamics of Decision Making

Having explored approaches to analysing a problem the reader is then introduced to the idea that there are three distinct steps to the process of decision making:

1. Defining components of the decision
2. Developing alternatives
3. Deciding.

First, we look at some of the reasons why making decisions in groups can be problematic. Here we look at why some groups or teams are able to create synergy in working together whereas others are restricted by inappropriate behaviours, political constraints and peer pressure. At this stage the concept of 'groupthink' is explored and it is shown how decisions can be made which are fundamentally flawed when working in teams.

It is shown how one should define the components of decisions in order to assess the validity of a proposal. This is achieved by the use of a Decision-making Framework which will ultimately be used to sift all the possibilities which might have been identified as a result of the analysis stage and the development of alternatives.

At this point we recognise that up to this stage we have purely systematic, rational and logical processes and that it is now useful to consider the use of more creative approaches in order to develop alternative ideas.

In looking at creativity we start by considering why our creative abilities tend to be stifled and we provide an overview of recent findings regarding creative thinking and the activity of the human brain. On a practical level we then go on to discuss various methods for capturing creative energy, including:

▨ Brainstorming
▨ Mind Mapping®
▨ Analogies
▨ Environmental considerations
▨ Visualisation.

Having used such techniques in order to generate more ideas which can be added to those which have emerged already from the more analytical process, we then go on to explain a process of deciding which entails considering all the possible solutions against the decision-making framework.

Chapter 6 — Managing Risks

The need to manage risks is considered as a three-stage process:

1. Identify the risks
2. Quantify and prioritise
3. Contingency plan.

The SWOT analysis technique is reviewed with particular reference to identifying and exploring threats either as things that could happen if nothing changes, and threats that might occur if specific opportunities are taken.

The practical application of probability theory is considered and the reader is provided with a simple method of quantifying risks by way of assessing the probability (likelihood) of something happening, and the consequence (impact) if those events do actually occur.

Chapter 7 — Practical Planning

In this chapter we consider the issue of planning and look at a number of different approaches which might be taken depending on the complexity of the project. Here we consider the need to identify specifically who will be doing what and by when, as well as the use of techniques such as:

▨ Backward planning
▨ Network Planning
▨ Gantt charts.

We also look at how, through the clarification of personal targets or objectives, it is possible to ensure that individuals are working in a co-ordinated way towards the achievement of the team or project goals.

It is recognised that by working hard in order to ensure that the plan does identify specific activities, it is then often found that monitoring and control becomes an easier process. Special reference will be made to the authors' continuing and published work in the sphere of target setting and goal achievement.

Chapter 8 — Concluding Overview

In this ultimate chapter we recognise that the ADAPT model is a systems-based approach to successfully institutionalising and managing a more strategic approach to problem solving and decision making. This final chapter aims to pull together the conclusions developed through the previous chapters.

1

THE NATURE OF PROBLEMS

In 'The Nature of Problems' we:

- *Consider some of the trends and forces which are affecting the way in which we have to manage problems and make decisions*
- *Suggest that most problems can be categorised as either 'open' or 'closed' and as such they call for different techniques and tools of analysis to be applied in working towards a solution*
- *Look at a number of approaches to business planning and dealing with strategic issues; and consider a framework for planning either at a business, team or project level*
- *Show how formulating a vision statement can serve as a powerful and bonding force behind which people can unite in order to achieve a common goal*
- *Briefly introduce the ADAPT model of problem solving and decision making which is then explained in more detail in subsequent chapters.*

Individuals in organisations are faced increasingly with the challenge of having to achieve more in less time and with less resources at their disposal. Additionally there is often a requirement to work with others in order to harness the creative and analytical ability of 'the team' in order to solve problems. In considering the case for a systematic approach to problem solving and decision making a number of external factors can be identified which are in effect driving this need. Here we will review these before looking at the different types of problem which people in organisations are facing.

The organisational landscape of today and tomorrow is undoubtedly quite different from that of the early twentieth century when the notion of management was first conceived. Historically, leaders and managers would make decisions regarding the future direction for the business and then use traditional skills of planning, organising and controlling in order to ensure that business objectives were met. Typically in the mass production environment, planning and forecasting would be carried out over the long term. The strict demarcation between the management and the 'workers', both in terms of their respective roles and expectations, meant that people were often seen as simply another cog in the machinery. Jobs could be analysed, broken down and compartmentalised. The rate of change was slower than it is in most industries and organisations today and therefore problem solving and decision making were quite different in nature. Managers or leaders would make decisions and rules and workers or followers would work in the way that their superiors determined. Contrast, for instance, the approach taken in the mass production environment of Ford in the 1920s compared with most of the automotive industry now, where the emphasis is placed on production employees working in teams to solve problems; it is now recognised that those at the operational end of the business are best placed to address such issues.

Another key trend which can be seen is the move towards working across functions, often bringing specialists together from different departments, even organisations, and encouraging them to work together to achieve outputs above and beyond what might be achieved by individual working. This, it seems, is symptomatic of the development of a number of specialist areas in many fields. Increasingly teams are set up to work on a specific project for a set period of time and it is expected that they will come together for a series of meetings, adopt appropriate ways of working or processes, and then produce their outputs or recommendations. In many organisations once they have fulfilled their project brief they are then disbanded or reconstituted in another form. For some the challenge of working in cross-functional teams, or alongside customers, suppliers, even competitors, is immense. Here there is a particular need to adopt a commonly agreed process or *modus operandi* in order to ensure that different abilities and contributions are captured in a structured way. Without such a focus on process there is a real danger that individual differences serve more as a handicap than as a strength.

As we have moved from an industrial to an information age it is apparent that whereas a common difficulty in problem solving used to be a shortage of information, the challenge is now related to the fact that there is so much information available. This now calls for skill in filtering and selecting information; one can search the Internet on any conceivable subject and receive masses of information at the touch of a button. Some of this information will be useful, some of it simply time-wasting; there is a need to be able to decide which is which and to use it effectively. Tools and techniques for managing information are essential.

Paradoxically, in this world of information there are in many areas of business and industry more unanswered questions than have existed in the past. As the rate of change accelerates, the body of existing knowledge decreases. For many there is a need to make decisions and to take risks in a calculated way, often sailing into uncharted territory; again this calls for a structured approach to managing risks and making decisions.

In order to gain a competitive edge organisations are seeking constantly to innovate and demonstrate uniqueness in their particular field. This means exercising creative talent in addition to drawing on analytical thinking processes. In the past organisations may have emphasised logic, uniformity and conformity; but now such qualities are being increasingly questioned. Those organisations and teams which are pushing back the boundaries in achieving their potential are doing things differently, questioning the 'accepted wisdom' and looking for an alternative approach. Such creativity does not always come simply as a result of natural talent; it is often as a consequence of creating the right culture for innovation and encouraging creativity in problem solving and idea generation.

In the more successful organisations which we have worked with we have also seen a recognition that there is real potential to develop the business by encouraging entrepreneurial skills at all levels. This calls for all to have an understanding of the business they are in and to be able to contribute by way of problem solving — there is a recognition that the most senior person in the hierarchy is not the person with the best under-standing of how to solve business-related problems.

This is in contrast to organisations where those at the more junior and middle levels of the structure are unaware of the business they are in and how their own work contributes to the 'bigger picture'. In our experience it is in these organisations where there is often an overemphasis on command and control, that initiative becomes stifled and the ability to harness the human potential of the organisation is seriously restricted. This can be seen in the case study of one organisation below. In reading this case study you might like to consider where you have seen similar examples of creativity and innovation being restricted owing to the development of a restrictive culture.

CASE STUDY — RESTRICTIVE COMPANY CULTURE

Brighouse Engineering is an international organisation which operates in the construction engineering, building maintenance and telecommunications sectors. It began as a family business with strong philanthropic values and remains in family control, though it has grown considerably to the extent that it is recognised as a key player in its more traditional construction fields.

The organisational culture tends to emphasise and encourage behaviours of compliance, conformity and rule following. Many examples of this were seen and selected highlights are shown below.

On one occasion two middle managers arrived at the start of the very same course that they had attended only three weeks before. When questioned by the external consultants about this they said they had realised there was probably an administrative error which explained why they had been sent joining instructions for the same course, but they did not like to question the issue so they just turned up. They would have been willing to attend the full course a second time had the consultant not suggested that they return to their workplace. Even then they insisted on telephoning their bosses to get permission.

A company rule was implemented to ensure that all men in the organisation wore the same company necktie. They were told that non-compliance would result in disciplinary action.

An emphasis on written rules and regulations, to the extent that on the head office site over 50 examples of signs and notices telling you what you should not do and over 20 telling you what you should do were counted in the company grounds and on the ground floor alone.

Furthermore, most of these signs were displayed in a clearly symmetrical fashion.

Several pages in the company procedure manual concerned how and when employees were to use the toilets.

Complex rules surrounding meal times with an emphasis on strict time-keeping and rules regarding who should sit on which table and to whom they should talk. One such rule said that you should sit next to a person you did not know and talk to them. Ironically, while this was designed to encourage communication many employees described how they were actually quite creative in getting around these rules. On another occasion a training session was being run for the top management team and a request was made for evening meal times to be delayed by half an hour so that discussions could continue. This request was declined by the member of catering staff who had to leave at a predetermined time. More surprising than this was the fact that the senior managers did not question the role of the catering staff in determining their own timetable.

Such rules and reliance on conformity were often irrational or difficult to justify but interestingly this organisation seemed to attract those who would not question the rules. The workforce are mainly time-served and feel a strong sense of loyalty to their company, and in fact people gain recognition and acceptance based predominantly on their length of service; this is a male-dominated organisation and the perennial catch-phrase 'I have been here man and boy' is quoted with pride.

Not surprisingly there is a lack of fresh ideas and resistance to new approaches and although some managers go through the motions of looking outside the organisation, as soon as alternative ways of working or operating are suggested they are very quick to explain why they are different and therefore why change is inappropriate. This has led us to coin the expression 'terminal uniqueness'; we felt that unless a significant change in culture was effected they are likely to become victims of their thinking.

Thankfully the number of organisations which are operating in the mode suggested by the case study above is reducing as awareness increases of the need for a more enlightened approach. Increasingly, it is recognised that there is a case for leadership not just from the top but from all levels of the organisation. Project managers have to lead their projects, team leaders have to lead high-performance teams, consultants have to facilitate change through people; these roles require the ability to work through problems with groups and teams and to formulate plans and solutions. Leaders exist at all levels, not just at the top.

Furthermore, there is a growing need for people to influence others without necessarily being able to rely on status and position power. Sources of power, influence and authority have changed. If others who we have to influence are not necessarily technical experts, and they are acting more as co-ordinators or facilitators, then there is a need to be able to demonstrate the systematic thinking behind proposals. This does not mean a strict adherence to a set of rules or procedures, rather that there is a need to show one's 'workings' when making recommendations.

THE DIFFERENT NATURE OF PROBLEMS

In our study of the causes of failure in organisations we have been able to identify a number of factors which apply in varying degrees, as shown in Figure 1.1.

Frequently organisations and individuals simply muddle through in attempting to address problems and make decisions. The fact that they do not work with a structured approach to

Factors causing failure	Extent of cause of failure %
Human error	12
Poor control*	8
Failure to define need*	16
Lack of system*	30
Ill-defined measurement*	15
Inadequate planning*	14
Other	5

*Denotes the fact that a systematic approach to problem solving and decision making can help to address the cause of failure.

Figure 1.1 *Factors causing failure*

define the problem and establish exactly what they are seeking to achieve means that they will often describe feeling that they do not have any control over their destiny. They will often say things such as:

'I am being pulled in different directions by different people/ organisations'

or

'I am so busy coping with the day-to-day problems that there is no chance of addressing long-term projects or developments'.

Without a structured approach to tackling problems these people are often seen in 'fire-fighting' mode and sometimes, of course, this is related to their preferred way of working; they feel that putting out fires or dealing with emergencies is more exciting than 'fire-prevention' or taking a measured and structured approach. In many management roles there is a need to tackle many different problems at the same time. The challenge is often broader than this though; several problems are frequently related to one another in undefined ways, some problems are more operational whereas others are more strategic, and it is often unclear as to which variables managers or teams can actually effect compared to those which are outside their control. For certain personality types the prospect of taking a structured approach to planning and organising can appear to be less interesting or active than simply doing something; indeed it might be considered that the 'just do it' or 'bias towards action' mentality which has surfaced in many organisations in recent years has mitigated against taking a structured approach to planning and organisation. Additionally it is often considered that taking a measured and structured approach to problem solving is really the preserve of the senior strategists and planners in the organisation.

We believe, though, that the problem solving and decision making model presented in this book can be applied at any level in the organisation, either by working through the full process described in a structured way, or by taking specific techniques and applying them to specific issues in a more spontaneous way.

Through the model presented here we will demonstrate how the problem can be defined in a focused way and we look at how a number of different techniques can be applied depending on the nature of the problem and the stage in the problem-solving process. It is important though in considering the subject of problem solving and decision making to recognise that problems can be broadly categorised into what we describe as either 'open' or 'closed' problems.

Open problems are very different in nature from closed problems and are not easy to define. Usually such problems are initially presented in broad terms which are open to interpretation. So, for instance, we hear comments such as 'the problem around here is morale' or 'we need to improve turn-over' or 'the problem is the competition'. As such, these

comments state the overall feel for the nature of the problem but in isolation they do little to clarify the detailed issues such as where the problem lies, how it should be tackled, or just what the required objective is in solving the problem. Furthermore, in tackling open problems of this nature there is no commonly accepted way of solving the problem. In fact there may be several ways of addressing the problem. Take for instance the previously quoted example of improving morale in an organisation: a number of actions might be taken to try to improve morale — improve remuneration, increase sales, offer more job security, address management style, to name just a few. With this example it is also particularly the case that the problem of morale cannot be disentangled easily from its context. The problem of morale could be related to local issues such as the management style of a particular individual or at a broader level to a recent reorganisation of the team. Furthermore there are factors external to the organisation which might well affect morale internally; for example factors as broad as the state of the local or the national economy might come into play here. Obviously some of these factors will be more within the control of those within the organisation who are attempting to address the problem than others. So with open problems the actual problem is often difficult to disentangle from its context and the boundaries regarding where the problem ceases and another problem commences are often unclear. These characteristics of open problems are summarised in Figure 1.2, where we also explore the characteristics of what we call closed problems.

Closed problems tend to be characterised naturally by many of the opposite characteristics of open problems. An obvious example of a closed problem might be deciding how to set up a meeting room before a meeting; the problem is easy to define and there are only a few options to consider. So, for instance, there is a recognised source of resources or facilities and the person who has to address this problem will be able to treat the task as a discrete assignment. At a more advanced level other examples of closed problems might include arranging to ship products to a customer or arranging a business trip.

What we have shown here are the more extreme examples of open versus closed problems; it is recognised though that some problems are more open than others rather than that all

Open problems	Closed problems
Problem is not clearly defined	Problem can be defined
No right answer — there may be many answers	Unique or few answers
Unclear method for solving the problem	Recognised steps for solving the problem
Cannot be disentangled from context	Can be treated as a discrete or separate issue
Boundaries unclear	Terms of reference or parameters can be defined

Figure 1.2 *Types of problem*

problems necessarily fit into a clear-cut and absolute category. It is important in looking at any problem to attempt to define the nature of the problem so that appropriate problem-solving methodologies can be adopted; we will show in Chapter 3 how to use the relevant technique of analysis for the nature of the problem.

APPROACHES TO STRATEGIC PLANNING

In recent years we have witnessed some interesting changes in approaches to strategic planning within organisations. From the post Second World War period until the 1960s the rate of economic recovery was such that there was a need to expand production. In a climate where competition was less fierce than it is now the emphasis in strategic planning was placed on being able to anticipate future growth some years ahead and then formulating appropriate plans.

From the mid 1960s to 1990s however the dynamics of competition became more apparent and strategies became more competitive. Strategy was focused on working out how to beat the competition. Strategic planning was the term traditionally used to describe an approach based on a belief that the context of the organisation is predictable. In this scenario effort would be put into working hard at managing and collecting data on a regular basis, say annually, and then making the right strategic decisions. Plans would be developed in order to provide resources and direction; and as long as the original predictions were sound then one could be reasonably assured of success.

What we now see though is an increasingly dynamic and changing external environment with massive upheaval socially, economically and politically. Traditional approaches to strategic planning are being called into question.

Now there may be more information readily available and certainly we are able to move information around at speeds which would have been unimaginable just 20 years ago. Paradoxically though, data which is collected today may be out of date or inappropriate tomorrow. This makes strategic planning in the traditional sense and long-term forecasting close to impossible; strategists used to collect data at regular intervals and engage in a top–down process of turning grand strategies into operational plans but now there is a need for a much more responsive and agile approach. In the past the strategists could set the direction for the business in the knowledge that any changes to the overall plan would be relatively insignificant as long as appropriate monitoring and control systems were established.

Now we are seeing a rather different model whereby there is a need to encourage those in more operational and customer facing roles to tackle challenges at local and different levels in the organisation, rather than expecting to be able to present an enduring corporate strategy which they simply execute. Such changes are requiring people at various levels to define their own vision of success, and formulate strategies and plans which are in keeping with the overall vision or direction of the business. This requires people at all levels and in all functions to be capable of contributing to the development of the business through the demonstration of entrepreneurial or what has come to be described as 'intrapreneurial' behaviour.

So there is now a case for the model of strategic planning shown in Figure 1.3, which has been adopted by many organisations in their top–down approach in the past, being applied by anyone facing the challenge of solving problems throughout the organisation. This hierarchy of strategic planning suggests that there are a number of key stages which need to be worked through starting with the development of a vision. The vision is a succinct and inspiring statement of the overall goal of the organisation, function, team or project. Often vision or mission statements are confused with marketing slogans. Such slogans might in themselves be quite helpful in presenting the appropriate public image, for instance 'We fly to serve' or 'Constantly exceeding customer expectations'. The real value in formulating a vision, however comes from the process of agreeing the content of the vision and ensuring that, rather than formulating a politically acceptable 'motherhood statement', the vision serves to unite those who have to work towards achieving it. In the next section of this chapter we look at some practical guidelines for formulating a vision statement and show how we have used a particular structure in helping a number of organisations and project teams to gain real value from producing effective vision statements.

Next in the hierarchy of strategic planning is the need to clarify objectives. In an organisational strategic planning process these tend to be defined in terms of overall financial targets or ratios and, while the vision states in words the long-term picture of where the organisation intends to be, the objectives tend to be

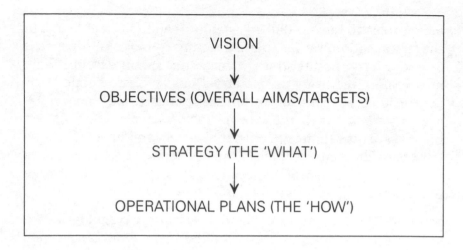

Figure 1.3 *The hierarchy of strategic planning*

stated in numbers and relate to shorter-term, say annual, targets. Included here might be objectives relating to sales turnover, return on capital employed or percentage of retained business. Of course in many organisations objectives might be stated in terms other than financial; a charity for the homeless might state that its objectives are to provide night shelter for *x* percentage of the homeless population. An environmental organisation might state that its objectives are to reduce a particular type of waste by a certain amount. An organisation responsible for raising public awareness of a particular subject might measure its objectives against geographical or demographic measures. So the objectives provide a succinct summary of the goals to be achieved and these objectives, when considered in conjunction with the vision, provide a basis for working on the development of strategies and operational plans.

The strategy part of this process is where the objectives are worked down into broad headings or categories and under these headings will be a number of descriptions of what it is intended to do. So broad strategic headings might be defined as follows:

- Financial strategy
- People strategy
- Operational strategy
- Sales and marketing strategy.

These are really broad groupings and the strategic headings will of course be different depending on the nature of the organisation or the project. Under each strategic heading are specific strategies which describe what it is intended to do in order to contribute to the achievement of the objectives.

Beyond the strategies are operational plans which describe in more specific terms what will be done. The relationship between the vision, objectives, strategies and plans is shown in Figure 1.4. Here for the first time we use the case of our own business, The Asset Partnership, in order to demonstrate the real use of the principles we recommend. You will see that throughout the book in many of the examples shown we work through using the same case study scenario. This will help to demonstrate how the tools and techniques of problem solving and decision making using the ADAPT model actually fit together.

By way of brief introduction to the business it is useful to know a few key facts regarding the market we are in and our history. As a business we provide an international consultancy service to a relatively small number of major organisations. The area of expertise is in the field of managing organisational and personal change and services range from direct consultancy advice through to the design and delivery of training programmes.

The business was formed in the early 1990s as the result of a formal merge between the two original partners in the business who had an existing strategic alliance. Since then the business has seen significant growth and faced the challenge of making the transition from a small entrepreneurial organisation to a more substantial entity.

Vision	We will provide a high quality, responsive and flexible consultancy service, aimed at optimising the use of human resources within organisations
	This will be taken in partnership and in a way which ensures mutuality of benefit for ourselves and our clients, and will be focused on the successful management of change
Objectives	Our success will be measured by the achievement of client business objectives and their degree of satisfaction at the services provided, as well as by our own business performance

	Objectives are set around the following areas:
	    Sales turnover
	    New clients
	    Retained clients/repeat business.

Strategies	**Product development** Development of new products to supplement existing training programmes. and for sale in standalone mode
	Financial Development of capital base and establishment of effective cost control and forecasting tools
	Technical Continue to develop technical resources and skills in order to retain competitive edge in speed of response and enhance quality of presentation material

	Marketing Develop focused approach to marketing with the intention of raising awareness through the development of public course provision and publications
Operational plans	(Extract of Marketing Operational Plan only) **Marketing:** **Public programmes** Develop suite of publicly advertised training programmes Ensure delivery of x number of these in the forthcoming year Establish relationships with network of conference centres internationally Build effective database for direct mailing **Publications** Manage through to final publication current projects which are partly completed Write at least two major publications linked to new training programmes and recent research Ensure publication in at least x number of professional journals Ensure speaking engagements at at least five major international conferences

Figure 1.4 *Extract showing the relationship between parts of the business planning process*

DEVELOPING THE VISION

As we suggested in the previous section, the development of a vision is about more than producing a set of slick words for the sake of public relations. Really the development of a vision serves two real purposes: first, to provide a picture or 'guiding star' for those who are working towards it to follow; secondly, the vision can serve the purpose of uniting and motivating teams of people ranging from the senior management team to more operational level teams. This process of building a vision might be likened to the analogy of scattering iron filings on a table top and then stroking a magnet under the table. What will happen is that the filings which were dispersed and pointing in different directions pull together and align in the same direction. In the same way, individuals in the group who may have held different beliefs regarding the objectives of the team or organisation pull together and align behind a common vision of where they are heading.

Here we suggest an approach to building a vision that we have used in working both with top teams in organisations and with specific groups such as cross-functional teams and product line teams. It is usually the case that when a team comes together for the first time there will be differing views held by the individuals regarding its goals and success criteria. Indeed where teams are made up of different functional specialists they are naturally more likely to view the objectives of the team from their own professional perspective; so a manufacturing manager will see production issues, a human resource specialist will focus on people issues and so on. Naturally such different perspectives lend strength to problem solving and decision making in teams if channelled appropriately. However there is a need to create a common vision of success.

Developing the vision may take some time and for those who are not involved in the process all they often see and hear is that the senior team go away on a fully expensed trip to a glamorous location and spend several days 'working' with a highly paid consultant only to appear afterwards with a piece of paper in their hands declaring proudly 'Eureka — we now have the vision'. For those not involved in the painful process of producing the vision this may understandably lead to some cynicism. The value though comes from those involved in the process of developing the vision spending time debating in detail their interpretation and understanding of the words which are finally selected for inclusion in the vision statement. In arguing about such issues the group is really deciding and arriving at consensus regarding what it stands for.

In formulating a vision we recommend that the team comes together 'off the job' for a predetermined period of uninterrupted time. Someone needs to perform the role of facilitator in order to co-ordinate the process. Each member of the group reflects on their own perception of the objectives of the group and privately commits these thoughts to paper following the format suggested below.

'We want to…	(an overall statement of the reason for the team's existence)
in a way which…	(a further statement which builds on or qualifies the first one)
in order to…	(a declaration of the outcome which is required)
as measured by…'	(how it will be known when success has been achieved).

This of course is simply a format for ensuring that the key criteria in forming a powerful vision statement are covered. In your own vision statement you may choose different wording but there are a few important points here. The vision should be clear and easy to understand and should seek to encapsulate the essence of why the group, team or organisation exists. It is strongly recommended that the members of the team work through the process of developing their initial version of a vision statement on their own. By doing this it is more likely that each member will actually feel more committed to stating their views. If this is not done and the vision statement is arrived at through group discussion alone, then what tends to happen is some members of the group, often the quieter or more junior, will be particularly influenced by others, often the more vocal or senior. This tends to inhibit potentially valuable contributions from being made.

Once individual statements have been produced each person displays his or her statement to the group and this is offered up for analysis and questioning by other members. What ensues is a discussion to agree the wording of a statement which expresses the vision for the team. The critical point to emphasise here is that every member of the group must wholeheartedly support the ultimate statement. This is a critical stage in the process of vision building whereby the real objectives of the group are defined and agreed. It is important for the facilitator at this stage to emphasise that before any wording is actually agreed by the group all members must be absolutely committed to such wording.

There are a number of quality checks which can be conducted in order to evaluate how effective the vision statement is. You might consider the following questions:

▦ Is everybody absolutely committed to every word?
▦ Have any ambiguous words been clarified?
▦ Are you prepared as a team to go public with the vision and be held to it by others?
▦ Does it create an exciting image?
▦ Is the language easy to understand?
▦ Does it conjure up positive images?
▦ Is it unambiguous?

So having developed the vision for the team or organisation it is important that this then becomes a real guiding force rather than simply an academic exercise which is then forgotten. Equally, if your team or part of the organisation which has formulated a vision statement is in a position to influence other teams or functions then the way in which your statement is publicised and used by others will be of particular significance.

It is clearly inappropriate, for example, to expect that the vision can be simply imposed on others and that they then will subscribe to it. We heard one manager in the head office of a financial organisation, for instance, say that he was disappointed that people in his branch network were cynical about the organisation's vision because a lot of effort had gone into 'hammering it down through the organisation'. The point with such an approach is that people have to subscribe to the vision, and as it relates to beliefs and values it is unlikely that people will respond positively to being told what their vision, beliefs and values are.

A more constructive approach in an organisation development context is for the top team to create an overall vision and then for teams within the organisation to engage in a vision-building process, as described above, where they create their own vision while ensuring that it is compatible with the overall vision. There may of course be some interesting discussions regarding areas of incompatibility and this may even cause some members to consider whether on a personal level they are able to commit to the vision of the team or organisation. While this may sound counter-productive, consider the implications of individuals within the team not having this discussion and how such differences might otherwise surface. This is what is often seen in dysfunctional teams where members are working to different overall goals and they subscribe to different values.

It can be helpful to develop a number of statements which attempt to encapsulate the organisation's values and beliefs; these are sometimes expressed as the organisation's values or pillars of belief. Of course, these will be very much related to the vision but provide the opportunity to clarify what the organisation or team stands for and, just as significantly, what it does not stand for.

So in the example of The Asset Partnership the pillars of belief have been expressed as follows:

- ■ 'Our success is built on continually satisfying client needs, and consequently precisely defining these needs is seen as a critical first step
- ■ The most effective way of working with clients is in a manner of partnership while taking an holistic approach to organisational issues
- ■ Our service must be flexible, responsive and expedient
- ■ In developing solutions, the emphasis should be on pragmatism, however this must be based on proven research or existing knowledge
- ■ Confidentiality is implicit in all our activities
- ■ Integrity is paramount in our dealings with both clients and suppliers
- ■ Our services must represent value for money for the client organisation
- ■ Solutions should be innovative and must represent the best of current thinking and practice
- ■ Whatever we achieve must be capable of measurement in terms of impact on business results
- ■ Linked to all we undertake is the requirement to transfer knowledge and skills into the client organisation; we do not encourage client dependency.'

Such pillars of belief say a lot about how the organisation or team sees itself operating and there should be sufficient confidence in them to publicise them, for instance to customers, clients and suppliers. This does mean however that others will be liable to hold you to your stated beliefs or values if you act in apparent contravention of them. So if an organisation states that integrity in its relationships with its suppliers is paramount, and you are a supplier whose bills are not being processed as per the agreed conditions then you might do well to quote the stated belief and ask for an explanation regarding the difference between the stated and observed behaviour! In a similar way we recently experienced problems in getting after-sales customer service from a major computer manufacturer which stated that its vision was to 'empower its customers through the use of technology'. When the hard disk on a computer crashed and we had a distinct lack of response in dealing with the organisation at a local level we asked the chief executive officer (CEO) of the organisation to explain why his organisation was having the opposite effect of empowering our business and challenged him to either change the organisation's behaviour at a local level or to change the vision statement.

USING THE VISION

So we can see from the examples above that the vision statement and the pillars of belief might well be used by others in order to question and challenge the actions of the organisation or team. Such challenges might come from within the organisation, for instance from other departments or 'internal customers' just as they might come from outside the organisation.

Additionally the vision and beliefs will help to guide the team or organisation as it contends with the challenges of moving forward. So, for instance, difficult strategic or tactical decisions may be made by referring back to the vision or beliefs.

At a strategic level The Asset Partnership was recently facing the option of reviewing its level of resourcing. The options were seen as: to grow organically by recruiting salaried personnel as demand increased, to build a network of associate staff nationally, or to bring in more partners to the business. A number of discussions were held before a decision was made but reference to the organisation's vision, values and beliefs helped. The last option was taken as it was considered that by recruiting personnel who had a stake in the success or otherwise of the business we would have the best chance of meeting our own objectives concerning flexibility, responsiveness and our spirit of partnership both within the business and in our dealings with clients.

On a tactical level, on one occasion The Asset Partnership was faced with a request from one client to deliver a series of training courses and at the same time to assess the delegates regarding their potential for promotion. This in itself would not have presented any difficulty had the client not suggested that the assessment activity should be covert rather than openly stated. In this case it did not take long to decide that such an approach did not fit with a number of our values and we then suggested that assessment was fine as long as it was declared as such to all participants involved.

The vision, values and pillars of belief should be reasonably enduring in an organisation, rather than changing on a situational basis. This does not mean that the ability of the organisation or team to adapt and respond to change is inhibited: by contrast the fact that there is an overall vision and beliefs have been considered, should actually help in making key decisions regarding change.

Even if the values and beliefs have not been discussed overtly it is interesting to note how these will exist and can prove to be a powerful force within the organisation. One is likely to be confronted most obviously with the organisation's beliefs and values when there is a clash with one's own personal values. This has been seen where, for instance, salespeople are required by their organisation to engage in manipulative behaviour and find this personally unacceptable or where young engineering graduates entering the high technology sector feel the need to leave the organisation because they experience personal difficulty in working on the design or manufacture of equipment for the deceptively named 'defence industry'. For those who feel a dissonance between their personal and their team's or organisation's values we have noticed that there tend to be a number of different behavioural or cognitive approaches taken. Sometimes the individual will take action and, as he or she invariably finds it difficult to influence or change the organisation's or team's values, this may mean leaving. Or the individual may attempt to live with the difference in values, but it is unlikely that major differences can be disguised for long; sooner or later the differences will surface and it may be that the organisation has to take action to exclude the person. Finally we have seen some interesting examples of rationalisation, where the individual actually makes personal excuses as to why he or she should continue to work in this environment. So the graduate in the defence sector may say, 'Well this organisation is contributing to leading-edge research which has more positive spin-off applications in the medical field' or 'They are a major employer in the area and they do provide employment for a number of supplier organisations, which is a good cause'.

So far we have considered some of the major changes taking place in a macro sense which suggest that problem solving and decision making are likely to remain a critical aspect of organisational life in the future. We suggested that there are broadly open and closed problems which we face and there is a need to be able to distinguish between these types of problem, not least of all because different techniques need to be applied accordingly. As a starting-point for organisations and teams we said that the value of the vision-building process should not be underestimated. Properly addressed vision building and the consideration of values and pillars of belief can provide a powerful foundation for subsequently working on strategies and tactical plans. Overall we emphasised that these activities should not be seen as the preserve of the senior members of an organisation but are equally applicable to operational or project teams.

In the next chapter we will move on to explore in more depth some of the major barriers to problem solving and decision making. By considering these it is then possible to manage such barriers and to ensure that they do not feature too predominantly when working with real problems in your team.

PAUSE FOR THOUGHT

▓ *How far ahead can you realistically look in predicting the factors which will affect your business in the future?*

▓ *How is strategic planning handled for the business? Is there a process which involves people at levels other than the top?*

▓ *How does the work of your function or team relate to that of the business as a whole? In what ways could this relationship be made more clear?*

▓ *Considering 'open problems' which you have to tackle with others, to what extent do you all have a common vision of success?*

▓ *What is your team's vision? If you have not formally engaged in a vision-building process then you might check whether you all have a common picture by asking individuals to commit to writing their thoughts regarding the vision and then compare notes.*

▓ *What are the values of the organisation or team? How are these changing?*

▓ *How compatible are the values of the organisation or team with your own values?*

▓ *How compatible are the values with those of individuals in the organisation or team?*

EXPLORING THE BARRIERS

'If knowledge can create problems it is not through ignorance that we can solve them.'

Isaac Asimov

In 'Exploring the Barriers' we:

■ *Identify the common barriers which often make problem solving and decision making difficult*
■ *Consider some practical ways in which these barriers can be managed*
■ *Consider those techniques which provide a helpful framework for structuring one's thinking when trying to understand problems*
■ *Explain how, through perceptual distortion, we often fail to see things as they really are, and show how this can create a barrier in problem solving.*

There is evidence to suggest that effective problem solving and decision making is often about successfully managing the barriers which tend to hinder individuals and teams. So here we will consider what frequently goes wrong and whether these barriers can be successfully managed.

Listed below are the five most common barriers to effective problem solving:

1. Not knowing where to start
2. Failure to understand perspectives
3. Inappropriate techniques and process
4. Need for a solution
5. Perceptual distortions.

These difficulties are now explored in more depth.

NOT KNOWING WHERE TO START

This problem is primarily the consequence of either a lack of understanding of the issue(s) or the apparent complexity of the issue(s) involved.

Clearly we need to recognise the cause of these difficulties, particularly if we are to select the most suitable way of managing such barriers. Let us begin by considering the first aspect which is to do with the problem solver lacking understanding of the issue or issues involved.

Sometimes we are presented with problems that are so vague or ill-defined that it results in not really knowing how to move forward. Some different examples of this lack of definition are shown below. These are examples of problems which have been described to us in the past:

■ Morale needs to be improved
■ We need to improve our efficiencies
■ I want to be a better leader
■ Our quality is not good enough
■ We are not adding value to our customers.

The issue here is that we know something about the problem and yet we would have to make massive assumptions if we were to proceed with trying to solve the problem rather than seeking to understand the problem more fully. Yet it is this very uncertainty about the nature of the problem that provides us with a mechanism for understanding the problem more fully.

In practice we have often found that we are able to define what the problem *is not*, rather than what it is. In these circumstances we suggest that you use the technique of a Problem Specification. This is shown in Figure 2.1.

	The problem is...	The problem is not...
What?		
Where?		
When?		
How?		
Who?		

Figure 2.1 *The problem specification*

With this approach you start by recognising both what the problem is, as well as what the problem is not. By asking questions such as What?, Where?, When?, How? and Who? we are frequently able to build a clearer picture which helps in defining the problem. Often as a consequence of looking at what the problem is not, it is possible through a deductive process to identify what the problem actually is. A worked example of this approach is shown in Figure 2.2 where we look at the broad

	The problem is...	The problem is not...
What?	General complaints about morale on the 'grapevine' Probably related to a range of issues	Related to recent business performance Just to do with pay
Where?	Manufacturing department Lower and middle level	In sales and marketing At the top level
When?	Getting worse over last two years	Two years ago
How?	Lots of employee complaints Graffiti High absence and unauthorised absence	Affecting customers yet...
Who?	Union officials and members	Main board members Head Office staff

Figure 2.2 *The problem specification — a worked example*

and vaguely defined problem of low morale in an organisation.

As can be seen in the above example, Problem Specifications are useful, but they only take us so far. Having gained a better understanding of the problem it would then be necessary to proceed with a more comprehensive analysis.

The other factor we mentioned above was the problem of the apparent complexity of a problem. Where complexity is concerned we often feel overwhelmed or unclear as to where to begin. In this case what is required is the ability to take the whole situation and to categorise issues in order to develop a more manageable framework.

A particularly useful framework to use is what we refer to as the Seven Ms; in effect this is a mechanistic checklist or aid that can help you to break down the problem and to consider the following individual parts:

- Market (market issues including the concept of the internal market and customer and suppliers within the organisation)
- Manpower (people issues)
- Machines (capital equipment)
- Materials (consumables or raw components)
- Methods (systems or ways of doing things)
- Money (any issues related to finance or money matters)
- Minutes (time constraints).

Where you are dealing with complexity the Seven Ms framework helps to structure your thinking and to make sure that consideration is given to all the critical items; however it is important to recognise that the technique as a system must not become a straitjacket.

CASE STUDY — SYSTEMS OR STRAITJACKETS?

We were consulting for a leading international business in the telecommunications industry and in particular were engaged in working with the Board of Directors who were undertaking their strategic planning process.

We suggested that the group should use a SWOT analysis (ie consider their relative strengths, weaknesses, opportunities and threats) and it was further suggested that the group superimpose the Seven Ms over the SWOT Analysis in order to ensure that they considered all the key issues.

The group then started to review their strengths and weaknesses against all the Seven Ms and we anticipated that it would probably take them between two and three hours to complete this process. We left the group working and stated that we would return in a couple of hours in order to review their progress.

Two hours later we returned to the group and were somewhat surprised to find that they were considerably behind our proposed schedule. The group had finished their analysis of strengths and weaknesses against both Money and Manpower but were apparently 'struggling' to find anything to say about Materials.

Their desire to use the technique had resulted in them becoming locked into using the technique rather than seeing it as a flexible aid which should help their thinking. In other words, the technique was doing more to hinder than to help their progress. Thankfully when this had been pointed out they were able to progress and they simply skipped the materials part of the analysis and moved on to analyse the rest quite effectively.

The above case study related to the use of a particular technique, the Seven Ms; however it should be emphasised that the principle of the technique system not acting as a straitjacket should be applied to any of the techniques we cover as part of the ADAPT model throughout the book. Techniques are proposed as a means of helping individuals and teams to structure their thinking and to ensure that problems are explored thoroughly; as soon as you detect that a particular technique is ceasing to do this then stop using it — try another technique or even a less formal approach.

FAILURE TO UNDERSTAND PERSPECTIVES

Here we are concerned with making sure that when we are exploring a problem we do so from more than one perspective.

Most situations or problems involve different people or groups of people who we might call stakeholders. These individuals will all have a view about the issue or problem but will tend to see things from a variety of different perspectives. If we are to be successful in finding solutions that are permanent then we need to ensure that all the stakeholders are defined and that we take time to reflect on their unique understanding of the problem as well as the needs that they may seek to have satisfied.

The technique of choice in this situation is a Perspective Specification; an example of this is provided in Figure 2.3.

Here we start by identifying the relevant stakeholders and then we start to complete the Perspective Specification by considering their different views and stances on a problem or situation. Of course we need to complete the section regarding 'How we see the problem...' and to set this perspective against the others. By doing this the subjectivity with which we often approach problems is reduced; it becomes apparent that people will see the very same problem in different ways depending on

How we see the problem...	How person X sees the problem...	How person Y sees the problem...

Figure 2.3 *The perspective specification*

factors such as their previous experience, prejudices, background, interests, attitudes, training etc. It should also be recognised that while a problem might be being discussed by just two parties there may be other parties with important perspectives who are not actually present. This is seen in the following case study where the meeting was held between the authors and the publishers but the perspectives of at least two other parties, the readers and the distributors, needed to be considered.

CASE STUDY — UNDERSTANDING THE STAKEHOLDERS

In writing this book it became clear to us that there are a number of stakeholders each of whom have a valid view of how the book should be developed. These were identified as follows:

■ Ourselves
■ Publisher
■ Retailer
■ Customers.

Using a Perspective Specification it soon became clear to us that if we were to be successful in satisfying all these vested interests then we needed to make sure that we recognised their differing views.

We realised that for ourselves the book provides an opportunity to summarise our current practices while at the same time producing something that could be used to support our training commitments. In addition, based on our previous experiences we knew that the book would complement our more traditional marketing activity.

Our publisher was not primarily concerned with the things we had identified as being important to us. What the publisher required was a piece of work that was academically sound while at the same time filling a perceived gap in the existing literature.

Retailers want to sell books, they are not primarily concerned about academic rigour but are more interested in issues of marketing related to such issues as the title or cover. In effect they operate on a principle that once the customer has picked the book up, they are half-way towards a sale.

Most importantly our research had suggested that customers are more concerned with the book being practical, full of no-nonsense tools and techniques that can be dipped into and out of as their personal needs dictate.

It was this understanding of different perspectives that enabled us to explore the problem of researching, writing and delivering a book that others would want to read.

As a means of starting to understand different perspectives on the problem this Perspective Specification approach can be used in a formal sense with a group or team trying to anticipate the perspectives of relevant parties.

Equally, If It Is possible and appropriate actually to ask the different parties about their perspectives then it may be possible to gather data directly without having to make assumptions. In a project management environment it is often appropriate to identify the relevant stakeholders and to enlist representatives from different areas who should work together in order to achieve success. In this scenario you might consider questions such as:

▓ Who is the final customer (external or internal)? It can be instructive to think in terms of a customer and supplier relationship when seeking to solve problems. Defining just who you are aiming to satisfy helps to provide focus
▓ Which functions and individuals will contribute to success-ful delivery of the project? Often different functions within the business have a part to play either directly, in support, or in some indirect way
▓ Which external contacts could have a bearing on the outcome? Often in problem solving there are external people or organisations which have a vested interest in the successful solving of problems or project delivery. These might include for instance legal and regulatory bodies or external suppliers.

A relevant analogy can be drawn with the situation of a manager trying to manage a sports team: it is important to consider the perspectives of many different bodies: players, supporters, financiers, local community and more. While all of these may be keen to see the team succeed they all have slightly different perspectives, all of which need to be considered. It can be helpful to consider the following categories of stakeholder:

▓ Direct members who contribute directly
▓ Those who are not directly involved but have an ability to influence the success of a project. These are often neglected because their interest in the success of a project is not always that obvious
▓ Customers internally or externally who will work with whatever the individual, group or team manage to produce.

Of course it may not be appropriate to enlist the direct support of representatives from all of these areas but it may be useful to involve some and simply to keep others informed.

INAPPROPRIATE TECHNIQUES AND PROCESS

In problem solving a common difficulty is that inappropriate techniques are being applied by those working on the problem. Sometimes this is due to a lack of understanding and focus on process-related issues and an overemphasis on unstructured discussion. In this 'free-for-all' environment it is often the person with the loudest voice or the most seniority who influences decisions and methods of working, whereas it is often the case that the quieter or less senior members actually have a more valuable contribution to make. Often members are inhibited by working with others of more senior status, though of course this will depend on the culture of the organisation and the extent to which people are encouraged to challenge the 'accepted wisdom'.

In one organisation a senior director described the amusing process by which decisions were made at main board meetings. He said individuals were in turn asked their views on agenda topics by the chairman, next the chairman would give his views and then he would go around the table a second time, at which point anyone who had previously expressed a different view to his own would take a few minutes to explain why they had changed their mind! In this sort of environment it is obvious that problems are unlikely to be explored thoroughly and with open minds and although a politically correct solution may be found, this is not always the best decision or course of action.

Additionally, more organisations tend towards the use of analytical thinking in tackling problems rather than creative thinking. Both approaches are needed, particularly in addressing broader more strategic problems. 'Left brain' logical and analytical approaches are important but used without the use of creativity are likely only to generate a restricted range of solutions. A common difficulty here is that as we reach so-called maturity we are often encouraged to dispense with creative thinking as it is assumed to be childish and to work with more logical thought processes. This is particularly the case in certain organisations — in our work we have often seen this in more technical environments. Also, this bias towards systematic thinking is seen in most large organisations where sheer size adds complexity and therefore increases the need for commonly understood and accepted systems and procedures. The value of child-like thinking, however, should not be underestimated:

'There are children playing in the street who could solve some of my top problems in physics, because they have modes of sensory perception that I lost long ago.'

Julius Robert Oppenheimer, Physicist, 1904–1967

There is a need for groups at least to be aware of the techniques they are using in solving problems. We have often seen examples of groups believing that they have used a democratic process of consensus building to arrive at decisions. In practice what we observe is a process whereby the decision is carried because of the views of the majority or even the minority or in some cases due to the self-authorised decision taken by one individual. In a similar way we hear groups talk about having used a creative brainstorming approach when in practice we see them engaging in little more than a discussion of ideas.

Clearly throughout the remaining chapters of this book we will explain not only the mechanics of how to use the different tools and techniques of problem solving and decision making but we will help you to consider why, when and where a particular technique should be used. It is this awareness of the purpose that a particular technique serves which is important: are you aiming to analyse, to create possible solutions, to use logic or to exploit creative energies?

NEED FOR A SOLUTION

In the fast-moving world in which many organisations operate there is a sense that solutions must be arrived at quickly. If a decision is not made then this suggests lack of progress. People are encouraged to 'do something — anything'. In problem solving this often leads to a pattern of problem solving which might be described as:

▨ Fire
▨ Aim
▨ Ready,

rather than the more measured approach of:

▨ Ready
▨ Aim
▨ Fire.

The danger with the fire, aim, ready approach is that assumptions are not questioned, alternatives are not explored, risks are not analysed and plans are not properly formulated. While this may give the initial impression that progress is being made it is often later on that the consequences of ill-considered decision making are felt.

Even when groups try to impose a more structured approach to problem solving and decision making there is a tendency to want to move straight in to finding solutions. Often people come to the table with preconceived ideas regarding the solutions and this restricts them in their ability to take an objective look at the problem and engage in a thorough analysis before identifying solutions.

Frequently the orientation towards solutions is exacerbated by the imposition of time constraints. For instance we see effective decision making compromised in recruitment where time constraints are imposed. Rather than wait until we find a candidate who meets the criteria set for the job, there is a tendency to recruit from those candidates who are available even though they fail to meet the specification, simply because they are available and there is pressure to recruit as soon as possible.

The other down side of rushing into decision making is that we fail to take advantage of what is described as the 'ah-ha' effect. This is where ideas and problems are allowed to incubate in our subconscious before decisions are arrived at. By allowing this incubation period we allow the subconscious part of the brain to continue to work on the problem while consciously we are doing other things or having other thoughts. Then when we least expect it a good solution is fired forward from the subconscious to the conscious and people often describe having experienced a moment of inspiration. While this is a powerful psychological phenomenon it is something which cannot in any way be forced. There is a need to take time.

Additionally where a group feels that it is making progress in its problem solving efforts there is often a reticence to backtrack and reconsider some of the assumptions which have previously been made.

PERCEPTUAL DISTORTIONS

Perception is the process by which we make sense of the world. We are constantly bombarded with information, and it is normally hitting us via all five senses. Just pause and become aware for one moment of all that is really going on around you. The chances are you will be hearing noises, seeing different things, even smelling, touching and tasting things. If you really concentrate on trying to absorb everything which is going on around you, you are likely to realise that there are things happening of which you were previously unaware. In other words you had been selectively filtering out data as a way of coping with the sheer mass of information.

Now consider the criteria you were applying in order to filter such information. You can probably put most, if not all, the filtering down to just two criteria: things of interest and things of threat. We are inclined to be more aware of issues which either threaten us or interest us. If you have ever had the experience of being in a crowded and noisy room and at the other side of the room someone mentions your name and you manage to hear them with surprising clarity, then this is due to the selective filtering based on criteria of interest or threat. Likewise, if you have ever bought a product, say a household product or a car, and then notice the same product everywhere you look, this is not because the products have suddenly appeared — it is more likely to be due to your selective perception.

Such perceptual distortions are especially relevant when considering approaches to problem solving and decision making. We do not always see things as they really are. Where multi-disciplinary teams are working together this is portrayed most clearly; the human resource person will see things from a people perspective, the finance representative will see the financial issues over and above everything else and the engineering manager is likely to see the problem from a technical point of view. Of course such teams are established in order to capitalise on the synergy which comes from expressing different views and opinions but it is interesting to see how people will often be biased in viewing a problem through their own eyes only.

Another common area of perceptual distortion concerns the primacy and recency effect. We tend to lock on to one way of seeing or judging things based on our initial or most recent experience. When we first come to meet a person or deal with an organisation we are likely to be heavily influenced by the impressions we form in the first few minutes. In selection interviewing we talk about the significance of the first four minutes. If we see someone as a good candidate in the first four minutes then our subsequent perception will be highly selective; we will look for evidence to support the validity of this first impression and filter out any negative impressions. This works equally powerfully with the reverse situation; if we judge someone to be a poor candidate in the first four minutes we will seek supporting evidence throughout the interview.

The recency effect works in a similar way but here we tend to be biased in our perspective based on the most recent experience. We see much evidence of the recency effect in performance appraisal systems where the appraisee is supposed to be appraised on the last year's performance but in reality is judged on their most recent project, good or bad.

Now in problem solving the same phenomenon is seen. We will lock on to one way of seeing things based on our initial or most recent experience. It is often difficult when you are locked heavily into working on a problem to step back and take a more objective view and to gain historical perspective. If the project has been going well for ten months and in the last two months has faced some real difficulty then there is a tendency to see only the problems and the negatives.

The other key area of perceptual distortion that can seriously inhibit problem solving surrounds what we describe as the 'halo' and 'horns' effect. This is where we will attach a figurative halo to a person, a function or an organisation where they display a strength in one field and we assume that they are strong on everything they do. With the halo effect the assumptions that they have all the answers are often flawed. Have you ever been asked for the answer to a problem you know nothing about but it seems the other person is considering you to be all-knowledgeable? The chances are that you have created a positive halo due to your strength in an unconnected field.

The horns effect works in the same way but the focus is negative rather than positive. How often do you see people stereotyped in organisations, where it is assumed they cannot realistically contribute to problem solving and decision making. This was brought home to us most powerfully in a consultancy assignment we were working on with a major international organisation.

CASE STUDY — DANGERS OF STEREOTYPING: THE 'HORNS' EFFECT

We were conducting a consultancy assignment in the bottling plant of a major soft drinks organisation and our brief was to spend a week interviewing various personnel, looking at systems and then to make recommendations for change. This clearly was an open problem and involved an intensive period of research in order to become familiar quickly with the culture of the organisation and the main issues which needed to be addressed in helping the plant to move forward into the future with confidence.

At the end of the week we had collected a mass of data and were sitting on the railway station due to return to our offices in order to write up our findings. Although the analysis was not completed we had, over the course of the five days, recognised many of the key issues which needed to be addressed.

A young man approached us in the coffee bar of the station and he was instantly recognisable as one of the employees who was working on the shopfloor of the plant; he had a short 'skinhead' haircut and his face, neck and hands were covered in tattoos. He approached us and mentioned that he had seen us in the company during the course of the week and he wondered what we had been doing. We duly explained that we had been carrying out some research in order to make recommendations regarding the changes the plant should make in the future.

His response was enlightening. He said 'Oh — that one again — they have been looking at that problem for years — you know what they really ought to do if they want to sort things out? They need to…'. He continued to describe a solution to the organisation's problems which considered issues such as structure, plant layout, remuneration and waste management and warehousing which not only coincided with the conclusions we were arriving at but went on to suggest more advanced solutions.

In due course we wrote up our recommendations in a well documented report and presented this to the plant manager who within a month had implemented all of the changes, including incidentally those enhancements which the shopfloor employee had suggested to us at the station.

We were left asking the question 'Why is it that it took external consultants to come in and make recommendations for them to be implemented when certain individuals within the organisation had the answers all the time?' We eventually came to know the tattooed character well through some of our subsequent work with the company and it became obvious that while he had the answers, the senior managers had never thought to ask him because of a strong tendency to stereotype him in his role as a manual worker and because of the 'horns' effect surrounding his appearance and some difficulties he had experienced many years ago in his social life.

So one should be aware of the various ways in which we as human beings tend to have our perception skewed based on various distorting factors. In problem solving, of course, we are normally seeking to take an objective view in exploring a problem and as such should guard against perceptual distortion. Many of the techniques we consider in the ADAPT model of problem solving and decision making are designed to help you to do just this.

PAUSE FOR THOUGHT

What problems are you currently working on which are ill-defined?

▨ *What could you do to improve the definition of the problem? Consider drawing up a problem specification as described in this chapter.*

▨ *Who are the various stakeholders interested in your solving the problem?*

▨ *What are the perspectives of different stakeholders with an interest in the problem? Consider drawing up a perspective specification as described above.*

▨ *How aware are the various members of a problem solving group of the processes they are actually using to make decisions? What could you do to improve this awareness?*

▨ *Can you think of situations where the quality of decision making has been compromised owing to time pressure?*

▨ *Can you think of situations where you have seen the primacy effect, recency effect, halo or horns effect at work?*

In the previous chapter we identified and discussed a number of common difficulties that might be encountered when we are engaged in the process of solving problems and making decisions. In raising awareness of these issues we began to consider some of the ways in which these barriers might be managed. In particular we explained the use of the Problem Specification, the Perspective Specification and the Seven Ms in providing a framework to help structure one's thinking. We also looked at some of the ways in which our perception is influenced by various factors and how this can have a distorting effect.

At this point it is useful to take a step back and explore the underlying reasons why some of these difficulties may arise. In particular many of these difficulties are related to issues of solving problems and seeking solutions in situations where there is a high degree of turbulence, uncertainty or change. Such a scenario frequently compounds the problem.

It is for this reason that we have designed and developed our own unique structured approach to problem solving and decision making, and because it evolved out of a need to manage in situations of high ambiguity, we have found that it forms a useful approach for problem solving in a number of different contexts. We have used the model in a range of different situations including the following:

■ Consulting with selected senior level strategists
■ Working with cross-functional work teams
■ Working with functional teams
■ Project management
■ Business process ré-engineering (BPR)
■ Organisational design.

The need for effective problem solving usually comes about as a result of some perceived difficulty or need. Such needs may have emerged for a number of reasons. Perhaps the business is being pushed into considering new ways of operating. Or it

THE ADAPT MODEL OF PROBLEM SOLVING

'It's not that they can't see the solution, they can't see the problem.'

GK Chesterton

In this chapter, 'The ADAPT Model of Problem Solving', we will:

- *Explain the necessity for adopting a systematic process when solving complex problems and having to make critical decisions*
- *Identify the relative advantages and disadvantages of using such a structured approach*
- *Provide an overview of the key stages of the model and explain how the model can be used in practice*
- *Consider issues of personal style when problem solving with others and present a model to help you consider the appropriate style of leadership to adopt in different situations.*

could be that a change in the direction of the business is presenting new challenges. In some cases where the problems are more strategic this has come about because of a broader culture change initiative. Whatever the reason lying behind a major problem-solving exercise we believe the following sequence of events to be critical:

■ Problem formulation
■ Analysis of the problem
■ Producing ideas as to how to solve the problem
■ Testing those ideas
■ Making decisions
■ Action planning
■ Evaluating outcomes
■ Controlling or adapting.

Our own approach subscribes to the above principles, however in particular we would define the ADAPT model as follows:

'A systematic and mechanistic process for the successful resolution of complex problems or projects.'

The constituent parts of the ADAPT model (Analysis, Decision Making, Active Risk Taking, Planning and Transition) are not in themselves unique. What is different though is the way in which the model is designed together to form a coherent whole. Rather than viewing problem solving and decision making as a series of isolated techniques we believe it is instructive to take an holistic view. With more open or strategic problems there is a need for a structured approach. In such cases it is common for there to be a number of differing perspectives to be considered and there is a need to make a clear distinction between them when one is analysing the problem, generating ideas as possible solutions or selecting particular courses of action.

The five principle advantages of using the model can be seen as follows:

1. It provides a point from which to begin addressing a problem and then provides step-by-step stages through which to pass. When starting to solve complex problems, individuals and groups often experience difficulty in knowing where or how to start. The model acts very much like a road map pointing not only to the start but also showing which way to proceed once the journey is under way.

2. It ensures a focus when working in groups or teams thus ensuring that all members of the group are synchronised in their thinking rather than some being at the stage of analysis while others are already formulating a solution. Often when observing a group or team engaged in problem solving and decision making it is seen that different members of the group are actually at different places in the process. Some may be engaged in undertaking analysis while others are brainstorming or creating possible solutions. The consequences can easily lead to mayhem and therefore the model does allow the group leader or facilitator to ensure that the team members stay focused on the relevant step in the process.

3. It gives the group a shared common language and therefore minimises misunderstanding regarding the process. The use of the ADAPT model does allow all the individuals who are taking part in the process to have a common understanding of what is happening. Many of the names of the tools and techniques which we have incorporated into the model are used liberally by other people and are often used with different interpretations. For instance, the SWOT analysis is used by many organisations and can be used in different ways. Similarly brainstorming is a widely used term but our experience is that it is applied in a range of different ways, in some cases with more rigour than others.

4. It provides a clear understanding for others who may not have been part of the process of problem solving of how the group or team has arrived at a particular decision. In showing others that you are taking a course of action it is often more persuasive to be able to demonstrate your rationale. Sometimes the external contact is the customer,

internal or external, to whom you have to deliver or convince that your decisions are soundly based. Equally, as we suggested in the last chapter, there are often a number of stakeholders who have an interest in your activity even though they are not directly involved and here too it can be extremely helpful to be able to show the methods you have used in problem solving. This issue would appear to be extremely important not least of all because we have often seen groups produce high quality output and then, having presented their recommendations to others, they have failed to gain agreement primarily because they have failed to show the rationale that has led them to their suggested course of action.

5. Finally, we believe that the model itself subscribes to the cognitive process that we as individuals pass through when we solve problems and make decisions. As a result we are more likely to adhere to the process and manage it to a successful output. Sometimes people will describe how they actually use some of the techniques in the model as part of their everyday thinking, and indeed they do; the model is essentially a distillation of the best practices in terms of human problem solving and decision making.

Despite the obvious advantages of using a systematic approach as suggested by the ADAPT model, there are a number of downsides which we should mention:

First, use of the model takes time and it is really designed to be used when we are undertaking problem solving of a complex nature. This should not be underestimated. Problem solving in groups naturally takes longer than working alone and if you impose the discipline of using certain processes and techniques as well then you can count on the time-scale being extended still further. However, by working in teams or groups with specific tools and techniques we are more likely to arrive at better quality decisions even if they do take longer than when one person alone takes an instinctive decision or course of action.

Secondly in order to use the model effectively it is necessary to have a clear understanding of the process. Hopefully having worked through the book and considered the questions raised by the Pause for Thought sections at the end of each chapter you will have a better understanding of how you can work with the model. Some individuals feel somewhat constrained by using such a model. It is important to realise that like any model it should be made to work for you. This means that you should be prepared to be flexible and use the process to assist you rather than allow the use of the techniques to dominate your endeavours. It is the principle of structuring one's thinking which is more important rather than having to use a specific tool or technique in an inflexible way.

THE ADAPT MODEL

Having considered the relative advantages and disadvantages of using this approach, let us now consider the overall framework of the key stages. We will then move on in the subsequent chapters to view each stage in much more detail including providing coverage of the practical application of the relevant tools and techniques.

Problem formulation

As can be seen from Figure 3.1 where the stages of the ADAPT model are shown, the initial step is to formulate a clear and common understanding of the problem. Here there is a need to identify where the boundaries lie and just what success looks like. At this stage we often ask individuals or teams to describe or imagine what it would be like if the problem was solved or no longer existed. Here the techniques described in Chapter 1 on vision building and in Chapter 2 on using Problem Specifications and Perspective Specifications can be particularly helpful.

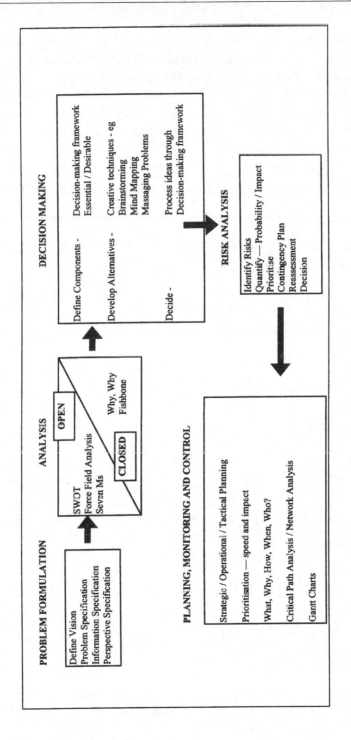

Figure 3.1 *Key stages in the ADAPT model*

In addition at this stage you might wish to use the Information Specification as a way of identifying what information is known in relation to the problem and what is not known. Having identified what information is not known it is possible then to decide in a focused way what information needs to be gathered before you proceed into the analysis stage. Equally, it may be appropriate here to consider the assumptions which are to be made given the lack of information. In working up an Information Specification you might use the Seven Ms to help structure your discussions (see Figure 3.2).

	Information known	Information unknown
Market		
Manpower		
Machines		
Materials		
Methods		
Money		
Minutes		

Figure 3.2 *Information specification*

ANALYSIS

The next stage in this model concerns analysis. We consider this to be the most important stage in the total process and the stage which is often neglected or omitted as people feel they are making progress if they are making decisions rather than analysing problems.

Analysis however should be seen as an investment in time. If analysis is undertaken correctly then the rest of the process in working through the model tends to fall into place relatively easily. If by contrast analysis is superficial or hurried then the rest of the process will at best be difficult or at worst will result in having to face the same problems at a later date.

Analysis is everything, yet many busy, action-orientated individuals are often much more interested in the solutions rather than ensuring that they have fully understood the problem. But what exactly is analysis and how do we actually do it ?

To put it simply, analysis is concerned with breaking or fragmenting things down into their smallest constituent parts and then closely examining each part. It is essentially about comparing and contrasting, identifying and understanding differences. All analytical techniques, irrespective of their level of complexity, are focused on analysing things in order better to understand the whole picture.

Of course our choice of analytical technique will be determined by our having identified whether we are dealing with either an open or closed problem or situation. Once this has been established it is then possible to select a way from a number of different options.

For open problems we would normally recommend either a SWOT analysis or Force Field Analysis, whereas with closed problems the techniques of choice would tend to be the Fishbone Analysis or Why, Why Analysis. These techniques are all explained in the next chapter.

Finally, it is worth reflecting on how long it might take to complete this stage in the model. Clearly this will depend on many different variables such as how big the problem is, which analytical technique is used and how many people are involved in the discussion. Some organisations which conduct a major analytical review of their business may spend several weeks conducting a SWOT analysis and this process may then be cascaded down through the organisation with each function or team conducting its own analysis following the major strategic review. By contrast we have worked with some teams where a SWOT analysis has focused on problems of a more specific nature and the process has taken three to five hours.

DECISION MAKING

Having successfully completed the analysis stage of the process we then move into the stage of actually making some decisions. This stage can be seen to be divided into three distinct steps:

1. Define the components
2. Develop alternatives
3. Decide.

The defining the components stage is concerned with putting together a framework against which we can test whether our decisions are valid and worthy of further consideration.

In many ways this is a kind of reality check in which we consider the limitations within which we are working and identify how we will be able to assess one possible decision against another.

It is important to note that this framework needs to be agreed prior to generating alternative solutions. If this is not done then there will be a tendency to make the framework or criteria fit the ideas which we have generated. Without establishing the criteria for decision making, decisions are often made as a result of personal subjective opinions.

The use of the decision-making framework has been recognised for some time as a powerful tool in the field of recruitment where the essential and desirable criteria are decided before candidates are shortlisted or selected for appointments. Here though we recognise that the same principles can be applied in developing more complex problem solving.

By this stage in the process the individual or group will have been using logical rational (left brain) thinking. However it is at this point that they should try to develop other alternatives primarily of a more creative nature. Brainstorming may be the technique of choice, however there are available an increasing number of techniques that can be used to help us to be more creative. In particular such techniques should lend themselves to spontaneity and should essentially be seen as fun. In Chapter 5 we look at the dynamics of decision making and consider a number of these approaches to developing alternatives including brainstorming and mindmapping.

Once a decision-making framework has been created and a number of possible solutions or actions have been identified, then the process of evaluation or actual decision making is relatively simple.

At the conclusion of this stage we can reasonably assume that we have completed preliminary decision making, that is to say we have made some decisions but have yet to test them out in terms of the possible risks that may be attached to those decisions.

RISK ANALYSIS

Where specific preliminary decisions have been made it is important to consider the implications of these decisions. Here we suggest a six-stage approach to risk analysis which takes you through from the stage of identifying the risks through contingency planning and adjusting the decisions based on the significance of the risks identified.

1. Identify the risks
2. Quantify
3. Prioritise
4. Contingency plan
5. Reassessment
6. Decision.

When preliminary decisions have been made it is important that we identify the risks that are associated with each decision.

Once this has been done then risk analysis can be undertaken to quantify and eventually to prioritise the risks.

Quantitative risk assessment is not really considered a precise science, more realistically its value comes from a group of individuals, after suitable discussion, ranking and rating each risk against two key criteria:

■ How likely is this to happen? (probability)
■ What is the consequence if this happens? (impact).

By using a straightforward formula it is possible to calculate the likelihood of failure. Once this has been considered it is possible to prioritise the risks and to go on to use contingency planning as a way of possibly managing those risks. Also the possibility of dismissing a decision at this stage should not be ruled out.

An additional advantage of conducting a thorough risk analysis is that it helps you to identify and tackle the barriers which others might raise when considering your recommendations. This means you will be prepared for the difficult questions which you might face if you have to persuade or influence others regarding the validity of your decisions.

Risk analysis can be a lengthy process, though if you are working in a group or team this process provides a good opportunity for splitting into several subgroups and conducting the risk analysis on various possible decisions in parallel.

PLANNING

Planning is essentially a pragmatic business and at this stage of the model we will provide a basic framework for undertaking planning where the emphasis is placed on who, does what by when. In addition we consider the important variables of speed of implementation and potential impact as a method of prioritising the order in which plans should be implemented.

Having formulated the plan as to what should be done, we look at a number of planning and control techniques which will help in managing and reviewing the implementation. Some of the techniques considered here, such as the use of a Gantt Chart and Network Planning, lend themselves particularly to monitoring and controlling in a project environment where a number of activities have to be carried out and a number of different parties are involved.

We move on at this stage in the process to focus on individual target and objective setting, showing how a structured approach with individuals should incorporate elements of the broader plans and will help ultimately in monitoring and control.

BRINGING THE MODEL ALIVE

As we explained at the beginning of this chapter, the model provides an ideal vehicle for using a systematic approach particularly when we are addressing complex problems or having to make decisions of a more strategic nature.

Although the model was originally developed with this intention in mind, it is important to recognise that the model can be used in a highly flexible way. That is to say it is possible to dip into the model and use specific techniques as and when they may be required. Indeed once you have become familiar with the total process and have worked with some of the tools and techniques which are described you will find that it is relatively easy to mix and match those parts of the process that most suit your needs.

STYLE OF PROBLEM SOLVING

Finally, it is worth closing this introduction to the ADAPT model by considering the issue of personal style in managing or facilitating a problem-solving activity. Style is concerned with the approach which we adopt as managers or leaders in problem solving and this may vary from directing and telling others to seeking advice or even empowering others to solve problems and make decisions with little managerial intervention.

What determines style? Of course personality is a contributor to personal style; however as personality tends to be difficult to change, we believe that in order to understand the issues that can be modified, it is necessary to consider two independent variables, the level of expertise which you have in the subject matter and whether the problem is more closed or open in nature. This is demonstrated in Figure 3.3.

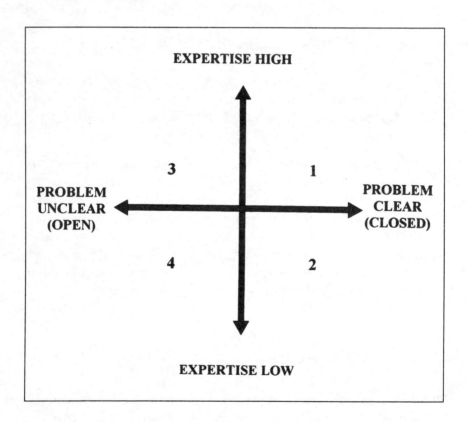

Figure 3.3 *The problem-solving window*

First we need to determine whether the problem is more open or closed. The issue of open versus closed problems was discussed previously in Chapter 1.

Clearly problems that are closed tend to lend themselves to more directive or prescriptive styles. We said that closed problems tend to be recognised by having just one or very few means of resolution and there are normally recognised ways of solving closed problems. There tends to be a right or a wrong answer or solution with closed problems. The following might be examples of closed type problems: solving a jigsaw puzzle, planning a route for a journey or purchasing a particular type of product. Admittedly there may be some scope for variation in how such problems are resolved but essentially this is limited when compared with open problems. In managing the resolution of a closed problem one can afford to take a more directive or instructive approach.

While by contrast, when tackling problems which are more open or ambiguous one would be less inclined to adopt a directive approach. Examples of open problems might be the need to improve business performance or to redefine a particular function in the business. Here there are no single answers and a number of different routes might be taken in resolving the problem. In this situation a more consultative approach would be appropriate.

So a key factor or variable to consider is how open or closed the problem is when looking at style in managing a problem. Additionally, however, we need to assess the level of expertise which exists among those involved in working on the problem. Where this is high then in managing a problem-solving activity it may be appropriate to adopt a consulting or empowering approach. Different members of a group will have their own valuable contribution to make and they will need to be given freedom and power to offer up their expertise.

Considering these two variables, open versus closed problems and high versus low levels of expertise, we have defined four different styles of problem management based on the window which we are operating. These four styles are described below.

Style W1: Problem Closed – Expertise High

This window presents the clearest choices in terms of personal style. Here the problem is more closed in nature — there are known and accepted ways of resolving the problem, and it may well be appropriate to adopt a style in leading this group which is more directive or prescriptive.

Style W2: Problem Closed – Expertise Low

Here the problem is also closed but the level of expertise within the group is limited. In this case a resourceful and open-minded approach will be needed by the leader. He or she should be prepared to look to others outside the group for suggested ways of resolving such problems and should encourage team members to be equally open-minded. So the style of leading the problem-solving activity in this situation might be more consultative or enquiring in order to find out from others how a particular type of problem should be addressed.

Style W3: Problem Open – Expertise High

Here we are dealing with an open problem and the group working on the problem has a high level of expertise. This might for example be the case if you were having to lead a group of functional managers in a major strategic business review. Due to the complexity of the open problem we recommend that the appropriate style when operating in this window is a combination of consultation and facilitation. The skills of consulting and facilitating will be important here as the leader will need to be able to capture the views of all members, ensuring that all members, including the 'quiet experts or specialists' manage to offer their valuable contribution. It may be necessary in managing this sort of problem-solving activity to take an assertive stance in dealing with the conflicting views and opinions of different experts.

W4: Problem Open – Expertise Low

Undoubtedly it is this window that presents the most difficulties both for the group and for the leader having to manage the process of problem solving. Here we have an open problem combined with a low level of expertise. We have seen examples of this sort of scenario where new cross-functional work teams have been set up in companies. They are representing their different areas of the business but are tasked with tackling issues which are actually quite new to them. They need either to acquire new skills or to seek support from outside the group.

People are likely to feel daunted by the challenge facing them; they may feel inadequate or that others are more confident than them and they often do not know where to start. Here as a leader you will need to encourage, coach and facilitate and ensure that the group is resourceful in looking to external resources for support, advice or expertise. Working on problems in groups actually provides a fertile ground for learning and as the leader you may see the opportunity to encourage group members to gain new skills and abilities and to acquire new knowledge.

We believe that increasingly people will be expected to operate in styles W3 and W4, dealing with open problems either where there is little expertise because the organisation is trying to break new ground or where there are a number of different specialists each with their own perspective on how problems should be addressed. Either way, for the leader of the group or team, problem solving in this 'open problem' environment presents very real challenges. We believe that the ADAPT model of problem solving, which we will now cover in depth, goes some considerable way towards helping you to face these challenges in the future.

PAUSE FOR THOUGHT

■ *Consider a group problem-solving exercise in which you have been involved recently...*

■ *How structured was the approach taken?*

■ *How clear were you or the group in defining or formulating the problem and how could this have been improved?*

■ *What level of analysis was conducted and how could this have been improved?*

■ *How were decisions actually made? To what extent was this as a result of an objective process?*

■ *What risks were anticipated before implementing decisions?*

■ *How open or closed was the problem and what was the level of expertise in the group?*

■ *How would you describe the predominant style of leadership of the group?*

APPROACHES TO ANALYSIS

'Who shall forbid a wise skepticism, seeing that there is no practical question on which anything more than an approximate solution can be had?'

Ralph Waldo Emerson

In 'Approaches to Analysis' we:

- *Consider a number of approaches to the analysis of problems and explain how different techniques should be applied depending on the nature of the problem*
- *Demonstrate how to use the SWOT analysis and the Force Field Analysis in order to expand our understanding of open or more strategic problems*
- *Look at two particular techniques for addressing problems which are more closed in nature, namely the Why, Why Analysis and the Fishbone Analysis*
- *Provide a method for prioritising problems which helps in deciding which problems should be tackled first.*

STARTING TO UNDERSTAND THE PROBLEM

In the last chapter we provided an overview of the ADAPT model which we suggested can be applied to dealing with major strategic problems. We believe that by working through the model in a structured way there is an increased likelihood that the issue will be tackled more objectively than by using more informal approaches.

Here we start looking at the key stages of the model in detail, starting with the stage of analysis. This really is the most important stage in the model and the one which takes the most time, though as we will see some techniques of analysis can be executed more speedily than others.

As a step in the process of problem solving, analysis is often given less attention than it should and frequently this is because of our natural tendencies to want to jump into generating solutions. We have worked with some groups where the group or individuals claim to have the answers even before they have been briefed on the problem; you may recognise this solution-oriented bias in your own organisation.

Also, once engaged in the analysis of a problem it is likely that a number of potential solutions will be generated through discussion and there is a danger that, rather than being viewed as potential solutions, they are seen as real proposals. So in a group discussion individuals will tend to want to hold on to their ideas or defend them rather than simply table them as possibilities.

The other issue with the analysis stage is that when a group is in the midst of a thorough analysis, say using a SWOT analysis, then they often start to feel that they are giving themselves more rather than less problems to resolve subsequently. They are right! Analysis in itself is very much about understanding the problem in more depth and this will raise additional or associated problems to be addressed.

ANALYSING OPEN PROBLEMS

In Chapter 1 we looked at the different types of problem and we identified that some problems are more open than others; we said that for example 'improving morale' in an organisation presented as an open problem. It might be considered open because there is no single answer or recognised route to tackling it, the problem may be related to other problems and it is difficult to disentangle the problem from its context. As such, open problems need to be analysed through a process of thorough exploration and discussion.

One of the most widely used tools for analysing such problems is the SWOT analysis which we describe below.

THE SWOT ANALYSIS

The SWOT analysis takes a structured approach to exploring the Strengths, Weaknesses, Opportunities and Threats presented by a particular situation. Many organisations use this framework as a way of reviewing overall business performance, where the open problem might be seen as the need to improve business performance. Indeed we would recommend that the broader the problem, the more likely it is that you will need to use a technique such as the SWOT analysis. The SWOT analysis is particularly apt if the people in a group tackling a problem are approaching it from different perspectives, because it ensures that all opinions and views will be considered.

There are different permutations of the SWOT analysis and here we will propose an approach which can be used in most problem-solving situations. While the experience of conducting a SWOT analysis is always challenging, the actual process is quite simple. First the group discusses the strengths which exist in a given situation. These are listed and some discussion will take place regarding these strengths. Be careful, though, that the discussion at this stage does not go too far beyond identifying and listing the strengths.

Next the discussion goes on to consider weaknesses currently existing. As with the strengths stage, the idea here is to go for quantity; to generate lots of views and opinions. As we will see when explaining the opportunities stage, the identification of weaknesses is as important as the strengths stage because a number of potential opportunities are identified coming out of the weaknesses. We have noticed that on balance a group will normally identify more weaknesses than strengths.

Having listed the strengths and weaknesses the next task is to generate a comprehensive list of opportunities. Opportunities might be gathered by considering each of the strengths in turn and then each of the weaknesses. A reminder is usually needed here that this stage is still about exploring or analysing the problem rather than building solutions. Opportunities are really just that — opportunities or things which could be done if it was decided subsequently to proceed with these ideas. The other key point here is to ensure that opportunities are expressed in a suitably specific way and are not simply general statements which cannot be worked on at a later stage. So a general statement such as 'to improve sales' would be considered far too vague to be able to work with; by contrast a number of opportunities might be identified which could have the effect of improving sales: 'To instigate an international advertising campaign', 'To launch a new product', 'To form a strategic alliance with a particular company'.

The opportunities stage of the SWOT analysis is the longest part of the process and groups should be seeking to generate as many opportunities as strengths and weaknesses combined. So each stage in the SWOT analysis so far is designed to expand the group's understanding of the problem. The leader or facilitator of the SWOT analysis discussion should be seeking to encourage ideas and views to be presented rather than withheld. If possible the actual paperwork which is generated should be displayed around the room as it is produced as this allows the group visibly to see the progress it is making and means that it is easier to refer back to previous discussions or to add further ideas into sections as and when they arise. This allows for an element of spontaneity in the midst of what is a very structured approach.

Next is the threats part of the SWOT analysis. We suggest that this can be divided into two sections. One is threats 'if we do nothing'. There will be a number of potential threats which could materialise if no action is taken, that is if none of the opportunities are acted on. This might include such threats as 'A major competitor could introduce a new product line which erodes our market share' or 'We lose so many staff that we are unable to maintain minimum production levels'.

Threats can also be considered from the perspective of threats which could materialise if we take action based on any of the opportunities previously listed. In part this is about identifying the risks which exist associated with certain actions and while we look at risk analysis in more detail later in the model it can be helpful at this stage to consider the major threats which exist.

In Figure 4.1 we provide extracts from the SWOT analysis carried out on our own business, in order to demonstrate in a realistic way the sort of entries which might be made in the different stages. Here the SWOT was conducted as part of a major annual strategic review and from this analysis a number of the organisation's strategies were reformulated and operation plans were instigated as suggested by the model of strategic planning shown in Chapter 1.

Strengths	Weaknesses	Opportunities	Threats (if do nothing)
Market			
Certain subjects being covered in training courses being offered are very topical Currently positioned as niche player in the market	Narrow field of expertise	Broaden repertoire of programmes to offer to the market by recruiting experts in other fields	Topical subjects could become dated

Strengths	Weaknesses	Opportunities	Threats (if do nothing)
Market			
Continued enhancement of international reputation through publications Future publications already written Publishers have international reputation	Long lead-time between writing and publication for traditional books	Look at different types of publication, eg open learning, own publications Link publications and advertising/marketing effort Strategic alliance with publishers	
Manpower			
All staff fully assigned to work in next 12 months	Little scope for taking on extra work if demand continues to increase	Recruit more permanent staff	Inability to meet future demand
Full order book for 18 months	Organisational size is small	Recruit associates with more informal contractual arrangements	
Much 'non core' activity is subcontracted	Secretarial and administrative support is geographically dispersed and involves several people	Consolidate administrative services (secretarial, mail shot, materials production) into one area	Escalation of indirect costs
Machines			
Exploiting technology	Limited technical expertise	Send team on externally provided technical training programmes	May make incorrect purchase decisions
No bureaucracy regarding capital expenditure	Currently running with two incompatible systems	Move fully on to new information technology system	

Figure 4.1 *Extract from SWOT analysis (continued)*

As we suggested it is also possible to look at threats from the perspective of threats which exist if we take the actions suggested by the opportunities. So, for instance threats viewed in this way might be expressed as shown in Figure 4.2.

Opportunity	Threat (if opportunity is taken)
Market	
Broaden repertoire of programmes to offer to the market by recruiting experts in other fields	May weaken image as specialists
Look at different types of publication, eg open learning, own publications	Would eat into time which could be spent on direct fee earning activity
Link publications and advertising/ marketing effort	No threat
Strategic alliance with publishers	No threat
Manpower	
Recruit more permanent staff	If demand drops will increase indirect costs with consultants unassigned
Recruit associates with more informal contractual arrangements	Associates will not be as committed as permanent staff
Consolidate administrative services (secretarial, mail shot, materials production) into one area	More vulnerable if this one person leaves
Machines	
Send team on externally provided technical training programmes	External courses may not be as relevant to our needs as bringing an expert in
Move fully on to new information technology system	Time-consuming

Figure 4.2 *Threats existing (if the opportunity is taken)*

This approach to looking at threats if a particular opportunity is acted on, simply allows the group to identify the most obvious risks which exist. This is by no means meant as a detailed risk analysis but it will help to ensure that further discussion regarding such opportunities is tempered with a degree of realism. More detailed risk analysis can be conducted at a later stage and we cover approaches to risk analysis in Chapter 6.

As can be seen from this extract of a SWOT analysis we have shown the analysis under three headings 'Market', 'Manpower' and 'Machines'. These happen to be three of the 'Seven Ms' which were mentioned briefly in Chapters 2 and 3. The Seven Ms provide a useful framework for considering broad business-related issues. To recap, the Seven Ms are as follows:

Market

Any issues related to the market in which the organisation operates. This might include for example thoughts on actual marketing strategies, market trends, advertising, consumer or customer activity.

Manpower

Consideration of matters relating to staffing levels, the type, nature and number of personnel employed in different categories. You might include here thoughts regarding manpower planning and the ability to meet future demand with current manpower. Also under this heading would be considerations regarding particular individuals.

Machines

This heading encompasses issues to do with machinery, equipment or any capital items. Consideration might be given, for example, to what equipment is used and how effectively, whether it is fit for the intended purpose and whether it will meet future needs.

Materials

Materials here means consideration of any matters to do with materials used in producing goods or providing a service. This could include matters such as what is used, sourcing and supply, quality and consistency.

Methods

Often it can be helpful to think about methods or processes adopted in carrying out an activity. Would it be worth using a different approach, could alternative technologies be adopted or could existing processes be improved? Many organisations have focused on the advantages to be gained here in recent years under the heading of 'process re-engineering'.

Money

Any financial matters should be grouped under this heading of money. This would cover, for instance budgetary constraints, cash flow, expenses and overall financial health. Current costs might be considered and areas for improved financial efficiency explored.

Minutes

In most problem-solving activity time will be a factor which should be regarded as a valuable resource. This heading of 'minutes' really is meant to enable groups to consider any issues regarding time factors associated with current or proposed actions.

So the Seven Ms essentially provide a flexible framework which can be used in a variety of ways. As with all of the techniques and models presented in the book we would emphasise that a pragmatic approach should be taken. In using the Seven Ms to help structure a particular discussion it may be found that not all of the headings can realistically be used; in this case simply use those headings which are appropriate in the circumstances. On occasions we have seen groups straining to find something useful to say under one or two of the headings where they would be better off spending their time moving on to the next stage.

We have now looked at an approach to the SWOT analysis which can be instituted when seeking to analyse any major open problem. As can be seen from the example shown above, the analysis does raise a number of additional, subsidiary or linked problems which may or may not need to be tackled at some stage. So having started with a broad statement regarding the nature of the problem, the SWOT analysis may raise literally hundreds of problems. The greater the quantity of information though, the more thorough the analysis was likely to have been and therefore there will be better data with which to work subsequently.

It is accepted though that there will not be a need for a full SWOT analysis to be worked through on every occasion. Some problems which also might be described as open problems can be more easily analysed using a more expedient technique which is called the Force Field Analysis. In the next section we describe how to use this technique and we take one of the strategies which was agreed as a result of the SWOT analysis shown in Figure 4.1 and show how the Force Field Analysis helped in clarifying some of the more tactical considerations.

THE FORCE FIELD ANALYSIS

The Force Field Analysis is a technique which assumes that the goal of the group is relatively clearly defined. Having identified the goal, a number of forces which are helping move you towards achievement of the goal are identified and listed. Then those forces which are resisting progress towards the goal are identified. The theory underpinning the Force Field Analysis is that every situation is assumed to be held in equilibrium by the forces in favour and those resisting. Theoretically all one has to do in order to achieve movement towards the achievement of the goal is to increase a positive force or weaken a resisting force. We recommend that actually it is appropriate to use this approach as a way of identifying a number of actions which can be taken, and as we will see in the worked example below there are often links between the positive forces which can be exploited in order to overcome the negative ones.

As with the SWOT analysis this exercise is best conducted with a group using a flipchart or whiteboard in order to serve as a common focus for the group. The structure for the Force Field Analysis is shown in Figure 4.3. Here again we have suggested that it may prompt ideas if the framework of the Seven Ms is used.

An outcome from the SWOT analysis we conducted within our own business helped us to formulate a strategy which meant

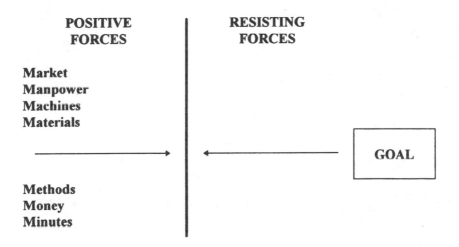

Figure 4.3 *Structure of a Force Field Analysis*

venturing into the market for providing publicly advertised management training courses. This in itself represented a departure from our traditional way of operating with a select number of clients and offering them training programmes on an in-company basis. We were convinced that strategically this was a good move but were naturally apprehensive because it meant venturing into pastures unknown and we were unsure as to how well equipped we were for the challenge. As can be seen from Figure 4.4, the Force Field Analysis helped us to understand the nature of the challenge more clearly and actually provided us with invaluable ideas of how to implement our strategy. We realised that while there were some resisting forces working against us, in fact there were also a number of supporting factors which we could exploit.

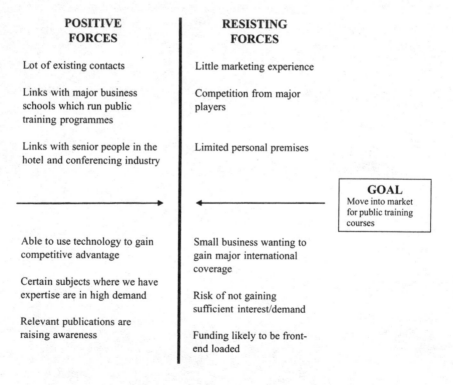

Figure 4.4 *Extract of example of Force Field Analysis*

So in order to use the analysis which was conducted regarding our venture into the public training programmes market, we decided on the following course of action. We recognised that we could draw on our contacts with business schools in order to ask their advice regarding marketing of public programmes. They were extremely supportive in providing information regarding pricing and timing of advertising campaigns. This helped overcome some of our concerns about lack of marketing experience.

We decided that we needed to develop a large database of contacts and we started by systematically organising our information on existing contacts and then adding to this so that we were able to mail shot in high quantities. Realising that there was the risk of not generating sufficient support for the early programmes by use of the mail shot approach to advertising alone, and that there was a need for such a strategy to gather momentum over time, we decided to offer special incentives to some of our existing clients in order to encourage them to sponsor delegates on the early programmes. We will show later on in the book how we used further techniques in order to manage the risks associated with this strategy and practically how we planned and implemented the launch of our public programmes.

TACKLING CLOSED PROBLEMS

We have looked at two approaches so far for dealing with the open problems which might be encountered by teams in organisations. Now we move on to consider two techniques which are appropriate for use in tackling problems which are more closed in nature. Both approaches probe in asking why a particular problem exists and to keep probing until such a stage that possible solutions start to emerge.

This is based on the Socratic approach to learning whereby we learn by asking questions. Young children tend to be very good at using this sort of approach to finding things out; they will identify a topic and keep asking 'Why?' until it is difficult for the adult to provide any more answers.

The two techniques described here, the Why, Why Analysis and the Fishbone Analysis, are similar in terms of how they work but there are slight variations by way of layout and structure.

THE WHY, WHY ANALYSIS

With the Why, Why Analysis the problem is summarised on the left-hand side of the page and the question is asked as to why this problem might exist. We say 'might' because these are not necessarily the definite reasons, only potential ones at this stage. Answers are then summarised in a column to the right of the problem statement. This might lead to a number of possible reasons. Next, each of these reasons is taken in turn and the same question is asked, 'Why?' This leads to another column and the process is repeated until solutions are identified. Normally we have found that one does not have to ask the question 'Why?' more than four times before a potential solution is found.

In the example given in Figure 4.5 we have again taken a problem which came out of our own organisational SWOT analysis and had been identified as a weakness which we felt we could address if we gave time and attention to identifying the root causes. The problem was that we felt our indirect costs were too high.

It can be seen in the extract for the Why, Why Analysis that by the time we had reached the third column we had actually identified a number of possible areas to be worked on in terms of action. So the possible solutions were seen as follows:

▓ Developing financial expertise
▓ Broadening staff awareness of business functions outside their own areas of responsibility
▓ Acquiring legal knowledge

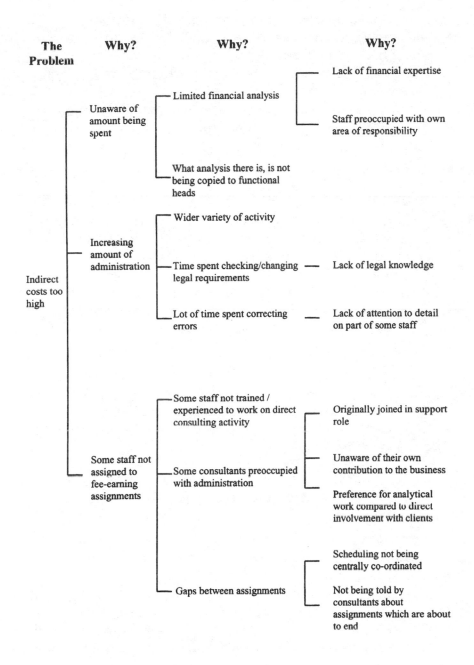

Figure 4.5 *Extract of the Why, Why Analysis*

- ■ Improving attention to detail on part of some staff
- ■ Increasing awareness of the contribution of different functions to the business
- ■ Appraising the match between staff strengths and the roles they are in
- ■ Setting up a centrally co-ordinated scheduling function
- ■ Improving information flow between consultants and administrative personnel.

These were not actually the detailed solutions as such. These really represent key headings around which a number of possible solutions could be identified. As we will see in the next chapter, the stage of 'Decision making' in the ADAPT model is where a range of alternatives are identified and decisions are made and it is in the stage of 'Planning' that detailed plans for implementation are formulated. It is worth remembering here the danger of being solution oriented; while possible solutions may be identified the actual decision making is another stage in the process.

The other word of warning with this technique, as with the Fishbone Analysis shown below, is that when working in groups there is a danger of the technique being used as a way of trying to rationalise the cause of a problem as lying with people or groups other than one's own.

THE FISHBONE ANALYSIS

The Fishbone Analysis is a technique of analysis which works in much the same way as the Why, Why Analysis. The main difference is in how the group actually lay out their thinking on the flipchart or whiteboard. Here the problem is summarised on the right-hand side of the page and this forms the fish head. From this the main spine is drawn and the questions are asked as to why the problem exists. This process is worked through in stages until, as with the Why, Why Analysis, possible ideas for resolving the problem are identified.

It is possible with this technique to use the Seven Ms described earlier in order to provide the initial headings on which to work. This is the approach we have taken in the worked example below. Here we took one of the problems which had actually come out of a SWOT analysis and worked on it using the Fishbone Analysis; for the sake of demonstrating the technique we have again only shown part of the full analysis (see Figure 4.6).

From the example of the Fishbone Analysis it is clear that there are a number of possible actions which could be taken to start to tackle the problems associated with sending and receiving goods. These might include the following:

■ Develop close relationship with postal service
■ Appoint person responsible for goods out/in and post
■ Update our database of addresses
■ Automate packaging facility
■ Change our details on databases held by others
■ Investigate alternative postal services
■ Improve purchasing of packaging material
■ Establish central postage budget
■ Improve planning of goods/post out.

So we have seen here two techniques which might be deployed particularly when working on problems which are rather more closed. These may be problems which have been identified as a result of a broader strategic analysis, using for instance the SWOT analysis or Force Field Analysis.

At this stage we would reiterate that analysis as a stage in the ADAPT model is really a stage distinct from decision making and while a number of possible solutions might be identified through the analysis of a problem, there is a need to recognise that decision making forms the next stage and should be tackled with an equally disciplined approach. In the next chapter we move on to look at the decision making stage in detail.

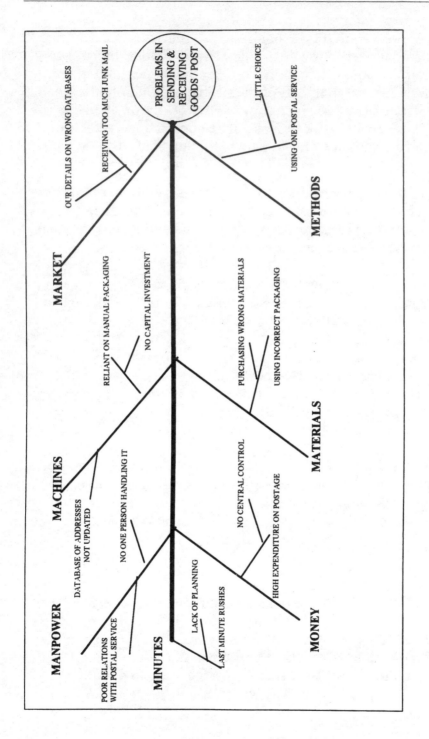

Figure 4.6 *Extract of the Fishbone Analysis*

PAUSE FOR THOUGHT

▓ *What are the broad strategic issues you have to address in your team, project or work group?*

▓ *How thoroughly and systematically do you feel you address these issues currently?*

▓ *Consider who you could involve in conducting a SWOT analysis or a Force Field Analysis. Are there people outside the immediate team who might have a valuable contribution to make by offering another perspective?*

▓ *Having conducted a SWOT or Force Field Analysis are there any more closed problems which you could work on using a Why, Why Analysis or Fishbone Analysis?*

5

THE DYNAMICS OF DECISION MAKING

'I am enough of an artist to draw freely upon my imagination. Imagination is more important than knowledge. Knowledge is limited. Imagination encircles the world.'

Albert Einstein

In 'The Dynamics of Decision Making' we:

- *Look at how decisions are often made in team or project situations and identify some of the barriers to effective decision making in groups*
- *Explain how to define the components for decision making as a way of ensuring that any decisions which are taken are realistic and practicable*
- *Consider how creativity can be used in order to develop alternatives which may not have been considered using more analytical techniques and in doing so explore the nature of creative as opposed to analytical or logical thinking*
- *Consider an approach to massaging problems as a way of seeking further possible solutions*
- *Show how the many ideas or opportunities which may have been identified during the analysis stage can be filtered and reduced to a manageable number.*

DECISION MAKING IN GROUPS

Decision making in groups is a complex matter. Not only do you have to contend with the difficulties of simply processing more data than if working individually, but there are a number of human issues which come into play. In theory the reason we work together in groups and teams to solve problems and make decisions, rather than working individually, is that better quality decisions should be made. The idea of synergy in teams suggests that the output achieved should be greater than the sum of the parts; so for instance a team of seven should produce a better output than the sum of the output if the same seven people had been working independently. Having said this, it is also the case that in reality many teams would be better off disbanding and working individually because of their inability to create synergy. Often this is due to personal behaviours which are seen in groups, which in fact are more disruptive than constructive. People in groups or teams behave politically, personality differences are an important factor and if the team is working in an organisational environment then it is likely that the relative position of team members in the organisation's hierarchy will have a strong bearing on behaviour too.

One key factor affecting decision making in groups is the style and behaviour of the leader. If this person is autocratic then he or she is likely to be surrounded by 'yes men or women' who will feel inhibited in making their ideas and views known. In contrast, if the style of leadership is extremely empowering then team members may fall into the trap of making flawed decisions due to lack of direction. So the style of leadership will need to be appropriate according to the nature of the challenge and the level of experience of the team members.

Many teams talk of consensus building, however unfortunately less teams truly achieve consensus. Consensus suggests general agreement or accord. The principle of consensus building suggests that all members of the group are given an opportunity to state their views and these are debated with the views of others until agreement is reached. Ideally there would be a full commitment on the part of all members of the group to any decisions which are taken. This is of course more easily subscribed to than achieved. The pressure on people to conform with the views of others in the group or, as we shall see below, with the perceived views of the group, is immense. This means that often what is meant to be a process of consensus building becomes a less rational process whereby decisions are actually made because of minority, specialist or individual views.

Some groups will set up formal processes for making decisions and it is interesting to see how often formal voting is adopted. Voting is in itself not a proven way of producing better quality decisions, but it is a way of making quicker decisions. Frequently what we see though are what might be described as informal voting processes when the group is actually intending to build consensus. Sometimes a decision is made because of an 'informal minority' vote where a minority of people support a course of action and because of their influence within the group their views are adopted. Sometimes the minority may comprise just one person or two people who identify in a group discussion that they subscribe to the same view and they make a 'psychological handshake' across the table. Similarly it is not uncommon to witness the 'self-authorised decision' where one person alone makes a decision and the group go along with it; this may be possible because of the person's personal influence, expertise or position of power in a group. Equally we see 'informal majority voting' where the majority view is carried into a decision, even though individuals may have strong alternative views but these are either ignored or not even presented. The actual benefit of such decision making being adopted should be questioned; these approaches do not make use of the full potential of the group or team.

The other phenomenon which can serve as a major disadvantage in working in groups is the concept of 'groupthink'. This is where a decision is made by the group but no individual would necessarily agree that they would have taken the same decision individually. This concept was demonstrated most powerfully, after the 1962 Cuban missile crisis when the USSR began building missile launching sites in Cuba. When this was detected US President Kennedy and his advisers imposed a naval blockade on Cuba and demanded withdrawal of the missiles. A warning was given by the US that meant for some time many thought we might have been on the brink of a third World War. When all of Kennedy's advisers were interviewed after the incident no one would own up to having personally believed in the decision which was taken on the part of the whole group. It was as though the group seemed to have a will of its own. With groupthink this is what happens; the group is cohesive, dissenters are intimidated and often there is an illusion of invulnerability.

This groupthink mentality is often seen in the corporate environment where inappropriate decisions are made for the same reasons; no one dares to present an alternative view for fear of being seen as nonconformist.

Another factor which frequently affects the quality of decision making in groups is to do with what we describe as self-oriented behaviour. This could include any of the following characteristics:

░ Dominating — where an individual takes up a disproportionate amount of time in talking to or 'at' the group
░ Blocking — where one person blocks the contribution of others by over-talking or ignoring them
░ Pairing — where two people pair up in order to give greater weight to their argument without listening to the views of others
░ Withdrawing — where someone either withdraws physically or psychologically from the group
░ Ridiculing — where a person makes fun of or attempts publicly to humiliate another person in order to enhance their own image.

So we see that there are a number of potential dangers in making decisions in a group environment. We believe though that many of the pitfalls described above can be overcome by taking a more objective approach and we will now describe the key stages of 'defining components', 'developing alternatives' and 'deciding'.

DEFINING THE COMPONENTS OF DECISION MAKING

In the ADAPT model the next key stage after the analysis of the problem is the actual decision making. The first activity in the decision-making stage we recommend is to do with defining the components of the decisions which will be made. This is the stage where the group is encouraged to think about and identify the criteria by which any suggestions (or opportunities in terms of SWOT analysis) are judged. Once these criteria have been defined the opportunities or possible actions are evaluated and effectively filtered so that only a select number pass on to the next stage. When working through a major strategic problem-solving exercise, this is often the most tricky part of the process from a conceptual point of view.

One way of explaining this step is to use the term 'reality check'; what we are doing here is defining the reality of the world in which the team or group operates. Here there is a need to consider the real constraining forces which are likely to affect any decision which is implemented. One way of expressing this is through a decision-making framework. A decision-making framework expresses succinctly both the essential and the desirable characteristics of any decision which is taken.

A good example to use here is that of the house purchase situation. If you went into an Estate Agent's office and showed an interest in purchasing a house, then the agent would be delighted; and even if you gave no more information than your current address, the next day you would be likely to receive hundreds of property details. More appropriate would be to find some way of ensuring that the agent actually carries out some sort of discriminating process in order to ensure the details of properties which are sent actually meet some minimum requirements. To achieve this you could list the essential and desirable characteristics of any house that you might decide to purchase. So you might draw up a decision-making Framework as shown in Figure 5.1.

Essential	Desirable
Money	
Maximum price £x,000	Preferably no more than £y,000
Location	
Within five miles of city	Within two miles of city
Within short drive (five minutes) to shops	Within walking distance to shops
Within three miles of schools	Within two miles of school Close to parkland
Size/building	
Three bedrooms	Four or more bedrooms
Medium-sized enclosed back garden	South-facing garden
	En-suite bathroom

Figure 5.1 *Decision-making Framework for house purchase*

In this example we see that there are a number of categories of criteria which are relevant to this particular situation; there are financial constraints, issues of location and matters to do with the actual property. The agent should now be able to offer a selection of properties which at the very least meet the minimum criteria. Furthermore because the criteria have been defined in a suitably specific way there will be no doubt as to whether any particular property meets any criterion or not.

When you then receive details of a number of selected properties you will be able to select further based on your desirable criteria; this will enable you to identify a realistic number of properties to view and then decide on.

The advantage of this approach to decision making is that selection is made against a consistently applied framework. So one is not, for instance in the house purchase example, seduced into selecting a property on the basis of simply an emotional criterion which applies to that one house, such as 'it has lovely French windows' or 'the neighbours seemed really nice'.

Now exactly the same principle applies to drawing up a Decision-making Framework in an organisational context. If through the use of a thorough analysis you have been able to identify many ideas for possible action, in other words opportunities identified from the SWOT analysis, you can then define your criteria for decision making and use the Decision-making Framework as an effective filter.

In Figure 5.2, we show how a Decision-making Framework was devised in our own business following the development of a thorough SWOT analysis. Through the SWOT analysis we had identified over one hundred opportunities which we could take and we had to find a way of working this list down to a manageable and realistic number. Once again the structure of the Seven Ms was useful, though we only considered it appropriate to work with a few of the Seven Ms headings.

In most organisational decision-making processes there are certain perennial issues which inform the Decision-making Framework, notably surrounding issues of finance and time. If you are finding it difficult to define the criteria for a Decision-making Framework, then keep asking the question 'What are the real constraints with which we have to live?'

There is a need to get the balance right in setting the criteria to ensure they are not so stringent that none of the ideas actually get through the filter. Equally they need to be sufficiently demanding to ensure that the number of ideas or suggestions are filtered to a manageable number. Later in this chapter we look at the mechanics of actually filtering the ideas using the Decision-making Framework.

Essential	Desirable
Money	
Must be within current budget. If involves expenditure should offer payback within two years Must be able to measure the cost of implementation	No capital expenditure No increase in costs beyond £x
Minutes	
Able to implement within next operational year	
Manpower	
	Able to implement using existing manpower

Figure 5.2 *Example of a Decision-making Framework*

If this exercise of defining the decision-making criteria is conducted at the appropriate stage in the ADAPT model, that is after the analysis, we have found that groups tend to find it difficult to separate this exercise from that of analysis. We would emphasise though that this is a very distinct stage, and you are recommended to try momentarily to forget your analysis at this stage while you define the criteria. Also you should beware the danger of putting ideas or suggestions down as supposed criteria — these are criteria by which every idea will be judged, not ideas in themselves.

Having defined the criteria for decision making the next stage we propose in the model is about developing alternatives.

DEVELOPING ALTERNATIVES

Up until this stage in the ADAPT model we have described essentially logical and systematic approaches to exploring problems. While a number of new ideas may have surfaced as a result of analysis, essentially these will have been developed through the use of logical thinking.

At this stage we believe it is important to recognise the potential of creativity. Using creative thinking it is possible to uncover ideas and opportunities which are simply never considered when using analytical thought processes. Through the use of creativity it is possible to generate a range of alternatives which can also be considered against the Decision-making Framework.

First it is worth briefly exploring the contrast between logical and creative thinking. In recent years research has shown that the two sides or cortices of the upper part of the brain deal with different kinds of mental activity. For most of us the left side handles mental activities which might be described as logical, rational and to do with analytical processes. By contrast the right cortex tends to deal more with images, colour, pictures, daydreaming and imagining things. In terms of our traditional education and training it has been recognised in more recent years that we tend to have inhibited or restricted creativity by focusing more on logical and systematic thinking processes than is beneficial.

If we look at the development of young children we will see how rapid their learning is in the first few years of their lives when creativity, or right brain thinking is encouraged. In the first two or three years adults perceive the creative energy of the child as a positive force. Imagination and fantasy is encouraged, indeed all the senses are used to encourage development — toys are noisy, colourful and tactile.

However beyond this very often the education system has encouraged compartmentalised thinking; it used to be considered unusual to study arts and science subjects for instance. Children reach a stage when their parents or teachers will discourage the wild use of imagination; it is seen as child-like, immature or inappropriate. Add to this the fact that when the adult joins an organisation logical thinking is given even more weight, and so it is hardly surprising that creativity suffers.

There are of course exceptions but these tend to be either more enlightened organisations or ones which are by nature of their business more creative, such as those in the media, arts or advertising worlds. So people are encouraged to fill in forms, follow procedures, obey rules, work within systems , all of which encourage logical and systematic, left brain activity rather than creativity. Those who do use creativity may be seen as exceptional, even eccentric or nonconformist. In some cases they will be excluded or simply humoured as 'a bit off the wall'.

Such predominance of left brain activity encourages people to think that we are either creative or not; one either has it or does not. This, however, is far from the truth. We all have the ability to use creative thought, the issue is that it is often restricted or dominated by logical, systematic thinking. Furthermore we may be restricted from expressing ourselves creatively because of social factors too: one may not want to suggest something for fear of appearing stupid or unconventional.

In using creativity though there is a need to become almost child-like, to free wheel, to dump one's thoughts without processing them first. It is from this sort of brainstorming activity that the germ of an idea may be planted which could grow and blossom into something much more far-reaching or profound than the ideas generated through analytical thinking. Many of the best inventions have been struck on in this way and many of the great thinkers in history, including scientists, have tapped into their creative energy as well using logical thinking.

Here we suggest a number of approaches to using the right side of your brain and exploiting your own creative talent. Some of these can be used in groups or teams where there is an opportunity truly to capitalise on the advantages of bringing several minds to the table.

RUNNING A BRAINSTORMING SESSION

Brainstorming is a frequently used term in organisations. Often we hear people say 'let's just brainstorm this for a while', however what we subsequently see is something other than a true brainstorming session. It may sound contradictory but even though brainstorming is a creative technique it does require discipline in terms of how it is managed in order to be effective.

Brainstorming should be used whenever you are seeking to generate a high number of ideas and want to try to identify alternatives which you might not have thought of using more analytical processes. We would certainly recommend a brainstorming session as a way of identifying alternatives if you are following the ADAPT model and working on a major strategic problem.

The session should follow this sequence. First, you should agree who is to be the co-ordinator or facilitator of the session and this person should take the lead by initially defining the subject of the brainstorming session. If the group have been engaged in logical analysis up until this point then it is preferable to find some way of breaking this pattern of thought and creating the right environment for a creative session. This could mean changing the environment, taking a break or warming up with a brainstorm session on a fun topic.

Normally the topic would be defined in the following way: '101 ways of improving our service to the organisation' or '101 ways of taking the business forward'. Clearly the heading needs to be sufficiently broad to encourage plenty of creative ideas but not so broad as to be meaningless.

Having defined the topic, the brainstorm session begins and the aim is to generate a high quantity of ideas all of which are listed without any detailed discussion regarding their merits or otherwise. The ideas should be listed visibly in front of the group in order to provide a common focus and to encourage trigger thinking. This works on the basis that if people are truly encouraged to verbalise their thoughts before they have time to process them, they are likely to be triggered by the comments of others. It is helpful if you can generate an almost child-like atmosphere by encouraging any ideas to be put forward, including the silly, absurd or irrelevant. It is often from these ideas that others are triggered into thinking of ideas which are actually workable and would not have been generated by analytical means. To this end it is essential that any evaluation of ideas during the brainstorming session is avoided and the facilitator has an important role here in stating 'no evaluation' when it does occur.

The actual brainstorming should take place for a fixed period of time. You will find that ideas start to dry up after a period and it may then be appropriate to draw a halt to the session. The next stage is to evaluate and group the ideas, using a more analytical approach. So the facilitator will seek clarification, agree with the group on which items can be ignored and pull out those ideas which are worthy of further consideration.

It should be reasonable to expect that a group would achieve a 5 per cent return on a brainstorming session; in other words if 100 ideas are brainstormed then five might be realistic to use and pass through the Decision-making Framework.

MIND MAPPING®

Brainstorming is very much a process that relies on group dynamics in order to tap into creativity. There are also techniques which can be used by individuals in order to work on the creative generation of ideas.

Here we would recommend in particular the technique of Mind Mapping®. In a sense a Mind Map® might be described as an individual brainstorm. When producing a Mind Map® the individual starts with the subject they are thinking about summarised in the centre of a page and then, working outwards from the centre they draw a 'map' which encapsulates their thoughts as quickly as possible without dwelling too long on detail. The more important ideas are shown as main branches from the centre and more detailed or subsidiary ideas are linked to these. It is also helpful to use colours if possible as this will help to encourage creativity and you might even wish to use pictures or images rather than just words. The Mind Map® approach works on the basis of working with the natural creative flow of the mind rather than spending time analysing one's thoughts before expressing them.

In Figure 5.3 we show a Mind Map® which one of the authors created when considering ideas to move his own business forward. It can be seen from this example that the Mind Map® actually looks rather messy on the page. However, as with brainstorming, it is possible to carry out the analytical process of relating the different parts of the Mind Map® and questioning one's thoughts in more detail after the Mind Map® has been committed to paper.

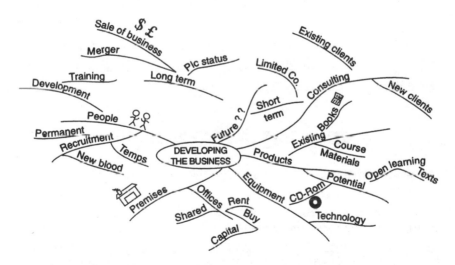

Figure 5.3 *Example of a Mind Map®*

It is also shown in Figure 5.3 how only one, or at most a few, words are written on each branch of the map. This is preferable to writing whole sentences, and makes it easier for subsequent use. It has been shown in terms of memory recall that we need only key words in order to prompt the individual to remember the original thought or idea.

If you are working in a group, team or project then Mind Mapping® may be appropriate when you feel that creative energy is drying up through group discussion. Again as with brainstorming there is a need to set the scene and create the right climate for it to work and it may be preferable to provide some practice or training in the skill of Mind Mapping®.

Mind Mapping® is a quite different process from the Fishbone Analysis which was shown in the previous chapter, even though the techniques at first glance may appear similar. Essentially Mind Mapping® is a creative approach whereas the Fishbone Analysis is clearly analytical and deductive.

So we have reviewed two specific techniques above, which can be used when seeking to exploit creativity; the brainstorming session which is a group exercise and Mind Mapping® which is an individually based technique.

In the next section we would like to suggest a number of other ideas which you might find helpful when seeking creative thought.

OTHER CREATIVE APPROACHES

Visualisation

In our own research we have found that certain individuals have a tendency to use visualisation in order to help them move toward the achievement of goals or objectives. So a picture of success is created in one's head or even committed to writing and on a regular basis the person mentally rehearses or visualises success. This approach to mental rehearsal has been known for some time to help physical performance in the area of sporting achievement and we have helped people to use a similar approach in the business environment through the use of imagery and what we describe as self-assertion statements. With self-assertion statements you define the outcome you are seeking to achieve and you write this down in a certain way; it should be written as though it has already been achieved, expressed in a vivid and inspirational way and in the first person. So an aspiring entrepreneur might draft a self-assertion statement as follows: 'I enjoy the excitement which comes from seeing and seizing new business opportunities every day'. By reading the statement regularly, and visualising success the picture is gradually imprinted on the subconscious and as a result the person's behaviour moves towards that picture. We have found that some people relate more naturally to such approaches but many use the same process, albeit on a more intuitive basis and in a less systematic way.

'What Would It Look Like If The Problem Didn't Exist?'

This is a question we often ask when a person or group presents with a problem and is not sure of what to do. Here we ask them to think ahead to the future and to try to create a picture in their mind as to what it would look like if the problem did not exist. To an extent this also draws on the ability to visualise or picture success. By mentally picturing success and verbally describing the picture it is possible to identify the circumstances which need to prevail. You could ask in more detail: 'What would be happening ?', 'Which people would you see involved ?', 'Where would events be taking place ?', 'What would you be spending money on ?', 'What resources would be needed ?', 'Who would be the main objectors — what would they be objecting to ?'.

Use Analogies

Again, as with many creative approaches, the use of analogies might at first seem less relevant or childish but this can be a powerful way of exploring a problem and thinking about it in different ways. In a group or team situation you might set up an exercise to work creatively on a problem by trying to liken the problem to a totally different scenario or context. So in considering the problem of bringing about business growth in an organisation recently, we asked people within the organisation to think about analogies and we presented a number of suggested ideas: musical instruments, types of vehicle, buildings, countries, animals. Individuals worked on this initially and then shared their ideas. The findings were fascinating. One manager for instance described the problem in the following way.

> 'As a business we really started up a bit like a build it yourself "kit-car". The business was little more than a hobby for one of the now Directors who ventured into it as a side-line from his other more important interests. He built it up in his spare time and added bits to it as he went along, sometimes adopting strategies which were little more than pure indulgence. Then it was as though the vehicle, or business, grew into something more powerful than anyone might have expected; we were getting demand for our product from all over the world. There came a time when this Director had to decide either to back out of the business or to throw himself into it full time. He took the latter option and along with the senior and experienced people he recruited he has built what might be seen as a more finely tuned racing car which has been competing more seriously.

> We must always hold on to our strength of being quick-off-the-mark and responsive to market changes. We see too many sluggish "taxi-cabs" and "buses" which are slow to turn, unable to change direction easily and laden with baggage in the form of bureaucracy and unnecessary rules and regulations. Like such vehicles they tend to be part of a larger "fleet" or group of companies where conformity is encouraged and they are often constrained by their regulators. We have to maintain our independence, we have

always been quick to learn and capable of taking almost any route to reach our destination; many of our competitors cannot do this — I suppose it is a bit like the buses which are unable to take the short cuts or the most direct route.

As we know with racing cars there is a lot of expense associated with maintaining the vehicle and ensuring that you are ahead of the game in terms of technical development — as a company we need to keep investing in research and rather like the racing car scenario we need to recognise who our sponsors are and maintain a high profile internationally.'

Interestingly when each of the managers presented their analogies this led to some genuinely original insights regarding how the business should move forward. Equally there were some constructive debates regarding the different perspectives of certain managers.

Create the Environment

It is essential if you are seeking to tap into the creative energy of people to create the right environment. It is most difficult to be really creative if you have been following a very logical train of thought or using some of the more analytical techniques we have been describing in the book so far. In order to combat this we would recommend changing the environment by either literally going somewhere more conducive to creative thought, or adapting your existing environment. Again the barriers to doing this might be psychological — it could be seen as nonconformist to hold the meeting in someone's house, in the gym, in the car or at a country club or in a winebar but the change of environment can change people's thinking and behaviour.

Many leading-edge organisations are now recognising that our emotions and feelings are affected by our environment and are reflecting this in office design. Included here are considerations of the use of natural light, sitting positions and comfort. Interestingly it has been shown that square desks and furniture tend to encourage decision making but discourage creativity. In some organisations previously unused space is being turned into meeting space for either formal or informal exchange of ideas. Some are redefining traditional concepts of the work environment, now referring to certain areas in their buildings as 'motorways', 'high streets' and 'market squares'. Some are taking seriously the effect of art, including for instance pictures, sculpture and ceramics, on the environment and consequently the thinking of their employees. Some Japanese organisations are using the power of aromatherapy to aid creativity and concentration. Our own experimentation in this area has shown that the use of certain aromas can indeed help with factors such as creativity and mental fatigue; our advice if you were considering experimenting in a similar way, would be to refer to a qualified aromatherapist. Some organisations in the West are now taking a more open-minded approach to such holistic concepts and the ancient practice of *Feng Shui* where one addresses the environment in order to ensure appropriate use of the energy flow and forces in a building or organisation.

Ask Someone Else

Finally here we suggest that one approach to gaining a fresh perspective and seeking alternative ways of doing things is to ask someone else. By this we mean venturing outside of the normal or traditional environment and asking people who you might not have considered as having a valid view for their ideas. You might include here, for instance, the general public, one's spouse or even children who are not so hampered with the constraints to creative thinking as adults. Remember you are not asking for definite answers here, simply seeking to develop alternative ideas and once you have generated these ideas you will then be able to process them through your Decision-making Framework.

MASSAGING PROBLEMS

We have considered a number of creative approaches in the section above which might be deployed in order to generate further ideas regarding possible actions. These creative ideas should ultimately be added to the list of ideas generated through the use of logical or analytical techniques such at the 'opportunities' emerging from a SWOT analysis. There is one further approach, though, that you might consider at this stage and which we refer to as massaging problems.

In massaging problems a number of basic questions are asked in order to facilitate a discussion regarding alternative ways of doing things. Often in problem solving we are so close to the problem that we fail to ask the almost naïve questions about why things are done in a certain way. Using the framework shown in Figure 5.4 it is possible to ask the basic questions without any one person feeling inhibited. Here we consider what is done, how it is done, when, where and by whom; you will recognise that these are similar headings to those used when drawing up an action plan, as shown in Chapter 7.

There are no hard and fast rules as to which part of the Massaging Problems chart should be completed first and the approach which seems to work best is for the picture to be built up through discussion and the chart to be completed by a facilitator who asks the questions as and when appropriate and subsequently completes the chart.

DYNAMIC DECISION MAKING

Earlier in this chapter we explained the process of developing a Decision-making Framework. This, we said, ensured that any ideas which are given further consideration, are considered against a common and agreed set of criteria. By processing ideas through the Decision-making Framework we ensure that only realistic ones are given further consideration.

	Currrent facts	Reasons	Possible alternatives	Review purpose
What?	What is done now?	Why is it done?	What else could be done?	What should be done?
How?	How is it done?	Why in that way?	How else could it be done?	How should it be done?
When?	When is it done?	Why at that time?	When else could it be done?	When should it be done?
Where?	Where is it done?	Why in that place?	Where else could it be done?	Where should it be done?
Who?	Who does it?	Why that person(s)?	Who else could do it?	Who should do it?

Figure 5.4 *Massaging problems*

The use of this approach is especially appropriate where there are a number of ideas being considered and when tackling more open or strategic problems and issues. The process of defining the Decision-making Framework can be quite difficult; however once this has been done the matter of decision making becomes relatively simple.

We would recommend that if you are working in groups you start by posting up your list of possible ideas or opportunities, which might be taken from both the analysis (SWOT or Force Field) as well as the alternatives identified through, for instance a brainstorming session, and then next to this post up the Decision-making Framework. You then start by processing the whole list of ideas through the essential criteria. Effectively, you are checking whether the ideas pass the first test if implemented. So this might work as shown below where we simply show an extract from a broader decision-making process.

'Ideas

- ▓ Run a national television advertising campaign
- ▓ Set up internal team briefing system
- ▓ Head-hunt new Director of Sales.

Essential criteria

- ▓ Must be manageable in this year's budget
- ▓ Must have measurable impact within six months
- ▓ Must be politically acceptable to senior management and customers.

Result of processing ideas

- ▓ Run a national television advertising campaign — idea dismissed — too costly and results not easily measurable
- ▓ Set up internal team briefing system — idea accepted
- ▓ Head-hunt new Director of Sales — idea dismissed as not politically acceptable.'

So in this example just one of the three ideas shown passes the first test of meeting the essential criteria. If you are working with hundreds of ideas as part of a major problem-solving exercise then you may have to manage time constraints in working through this decision-making process. In this case we would recommend a fun way of speeding up the process which can be quite dynamic. The essential criteria are divided up and allocated to certain individuals in the group and then as each item is processed that person is asked to state 'yes' or 'no' as to whether the idea is to be accepted. In this way it is possible to process hundreds of ideas in a short space of time.

So by working through the essential criteria you will have reduced the number of ideas substantially; as we said earlier though, the effectiveness of the filtering will depend on how well defined the criteria are — the tighter the criteria the fewer ideas will pass through, the looser the criteria then more ideas will pass through. The next stage is the second part of the filtering process whereby you follow the same process but now check whether the ideas which have passed through the essential criteria actually satisfy the desirable criteria. This in effect is a way of discriminating still further and may or may not be necessary depending on the number of ideas passing through the essentials filter.

In the ADAPT model then, we have now reached the stage of making a number of decisions as to what we would like to do. There is though another key stage which we will move on to explore in the next chapter, which is about identifying and managing the risks associated with these actions.

PAUSE FOR THOUGHT

▓ *What is the style of leadership in your group or team? Is it more autocratic or empowering?*

▓ *What effect does this have on the level of contribution of different members?*

▓ *How are decisions made in your team, group or project? Do you use, for instance, predominantly majority voting, minority voting or consensus building?*

▓ *To what extent to you see the following self-oriented behaviours in groups?*
— *Dominating*
— *Blocking*
— *Pairing*
— *Special interest pleading*
— *Withdrawing*
— *Ridiculing*

▓ *To what extent does your organisation, team or project encourage creative thinking? What more could be done?*

▓ *How conducive is the environment to creative thinking? What about the use of offices, common space, meeting areas, facilities, light, space, music, furniture etc?*

▓ *Practise drawing up a Mind Map® choosing a subject of interest from either work or outside your work environment.*

MANAGING RISKS

'Fools rush in where angels fear to tread.'

Alexander Pope

In 'Managing Risks' we will:

- *Build on the previous chapters related to the stages in the ADAPT model of analysis and decision making*
- *Discuss the issue of risk and recognise the need to manage risk in order to ensure our overall success and to anticipate potential difficulties*
- *Consider how risks can be identified and described*
- *Demonstrate a way of quantifying risks by considering the probability and impact of risks and show how this can lead us into being able to prioritise risks as a prerequisite to their effective management*
- *Discuss the notion of contingency planning as a consequence of risk analysis.*

RISK ANALYSIS

In the previous chapters we have looked at the way in which through systematic analysis it is possible to identify opportunities or potential solutions to problems. We saw that by using the Decision-making Framework it is possible to check whether these ideas or opportunities pass a basic reality check, in other words are consistent with our eventual goals.

So, up to this point we have completed the analysis, generated numerous potential solutions and undertaken an objective evaluation to see if these solutions are in line with our overall goals and the reality of the constraints with which we have to live.

It is important to note that at this point that we have not moved into implementation mode. Often at this stage we see groups starting really to believe in their potential solutions. This is of course encouraging and to be expected but there is a danger here that groups start jumping straight into the implementation stage. It is necessary for discipline to be applied in order to ensure that ideas are not implemented at this stage without any risk analysis; indeed there may be possible ideas or solutions about which we feel strongly; however such decisions are still only tentative at this time and should remain so until we have completed an appraisal of both the obvious and less obvious risks.

Risk analysis is not a glamorous activity and to some people it may even be seen as negative or as tempting fate. However, by anticipating difficulties which might arise with the implementation of suggested solutions it is often found that there is a need to reconsider these proposals and either make critical changes or plan implementation in such a way that the risks are diminished.

The other major advantage of conducting a thorough risk analysis before moving into implementation is in further exploring ideas which actually appear somewhat adventurous or too risky to receive approval or acceptance. Additionally a thorough risk analysis will help in building a persuasive case for implementing a recommendation.

As a starting point it is useful to consider what we mean by risk. Within the context of the ADAPT model we would define risk as follows:

'Those factors that could conspire to restrict or hinder successful implementation of a particular course of action.'

In order to manage risks successfully it is important to recognise that several steps are necessary:

▨ Identify the risks
▨ Quantify
▨ Prioritise
▨ Contingency plan
▨ Reassessment
▨ Decision.

If we have been using the SWOT analysis as the main analytical technique for analysing a major open problem then a great number of risks will have been identified in the process of working through the threats section. In this case the only remaining consideration is to identify risks which emerge from the output of any creative approach which may have been taken to 'developing alternatives' as described in the last chapter.

Identifying actual risks is a relatively straightforward process. We suggest that the easiest way to accomplish this is by listing the additional possible actions or strategies which might have come from, for instance, a brainstorming session, and then through discussion and debate to develop a list of associated risks.

If you have not used the full SWOT analysis approach and have by preference chosen to use either a Force Field Analysis or even some of the closed analytical techniques, then it is likely that the process of defining the risks will take longer because no consideration will have been given to these risks up to this point.

Again, the structure afforded by the Seven Ms can be helpful. You start by listing the possible ideas or solutions down one side of the page and then using the Seven M headings you discuss and agree the possible risks. An example of this is shown in Figure 6.1. Here we have taken the example which was discussed earlier in the book of The Asset Partnership deciding to venture into the market for the delivery of public training programmes having to date concentrated on working with selected clients.

Proposed action	Seven Ms	Risks
Develop business by expanding into the market for the delivery of public training	Market	This is a new market for us and the competition is not fully understood. Risk of market being flooded with similar products. By contrast may create demand we cannot meet
	Manpower	May not have sufficient manpower to manage administration
	Machines	Do not have sufficient technology to run major database. Risk also of database becoming out of date Also may not have sufficient hardware for delivery of courses
	Materials	No obvious risks
	Methods	Could lead to bureaucracy
	Money	Having to front-end load funding of such a project — could run out of funds unless generate sufficient delegates to make the project pay Could get pricing of courses wrong and fail to attract interest
	Minutes	Not sufficient time given our other commitments

Figure 6.1 *Listing the risks*

Once all the risks have been identified then the next stage of the process is to quantify the extent to which that risk presents a potential threat. In doing this we recognise that there are two critical variables in risk assessment: probability and impact.

Probability

Probability is concerned with chance or the likelihood that a particular risk or threat will arise. In using this approach we should look at each potential risk and should ask ourselves the following question: 'How likely is it that this will become a problem?'

Having considered and discussed this question it is then necessary to use judgement to weight the strength of the probability of the risk materialising. This is not a precise science, however often through good debate a group can fairly accurately reach a consensus as to the extent of the likelihood that something may or may not happen.

As our approach is essentially based on the concepts of probability theory; when weighting each risk we recommend that you use a scale of 0–1, where 1 represents a 100 per cent certainty that something, in this case the risk, will materialise.

Naturally some risks will have a high probability whereas others will tend to be less likely to happen, however it is important to remember that at this point we are only considering the factor of probability or likelihood. Once this has been completed we can move on to consider the second important variable.

Impact

Impact is concerned with the consequences of something happening and the way in which it will affect our overall plan. When considering the issue of impact it is useful to ask the following question: 'If this happens to what extent will it prevent us from achieving our goal?'

As with probability it is necessary that you try to quantify this question by discussion and debate. Ultimately you weight your response this time using a scale of 0–10 where 10 represents total disaster or total negative impact on the project. Note that the higher the score the worse the situation; there is potential for groups to become confused at this stage so keep in mind that you are assessing the risk of something negative happening.

Once both probability and impact have been quantified we would recommend that you multiply both scores together to produce an overall quantitative assessment of the risks. A worked example of the quantifying stage of risk analysis is shown in Figure 6.2.

Seven Ms	Risks	Probability (0–1)	Impact (0–10)	Total
Market	Risk of market being flooded with similar products	0.5	7	3.5
	By contrast we may create demand we cannot meet	0.3	4	1.2
Manpower	May not have sufficient manpower to manage administration	0.7	3	2.1
Machines	Do not have sufficient technology to run major database	0.7	8	5.6
	Risk also of database becoming out of date	0.9	9	8.1
	Also may not have sufficient hardware/equipment for delivery of courses	0.4	4	1.6
Methods	Could lead to bureaucracy	0.3	5	1.5
Money	Having to front-end load funding of such a project — could run out of funds unless generate sufficient delegates to make the project pay	0.9	9	8.1
	Could get pricing of courses wrong and fail to attract interest	0.5	7	3.5
Minutes	Not sufficient time given our other commitments	0.3	6	1.8

Figure 6.2 *Quantifying the risks*

So, as you can see in the worked example in Figure 6.2 of the quantifying stage of risk analysis, some risk factors have come out as especially significant and therefore worthy of attention before proceeding with the action. In particular the difficulties of the project being front-end loaded in terms of costs appears to present a real risk which could jeopardise the project. Similarly it appears that the risk of the database, which is used for mail-shot advertising, becoming out of date would threaten the viability of this effort.

By contrast certain risks present much less of an overall threat and while they should not be ignored they do not warrant so much attention as the high risk items. So, for example, the danger of creating so much demand that we could not meet it was judged as less of a risk primarily because this is considered to be a high quality problem and if it did arise it could be resolved by increasing the level of resourcing.

So having quantified the risks associated with a particular course of action it is now possible to prioritise which particular risks are to be addressed proactively if you decide to continue with pursuing the proposed idea. Here there is a need to decide a particular threshold above which it is considered too risky to proceed and above which the risk has to be managed actively.

Clearly, despite the fact there will still be an element of subjectivity in this process it does force the group to stand back and consider risks more objectively than would be the case if no predetermined process such as that described is adopted.

Having now assessed the risks associated with a particular course of action the next step is to assess whether such risks are acceptable and what actions are necessary to negate or minimise such risks.

Before we move on to look at contingency planning as part of risk analysis it should be mentioned that in the example shown in Figure 6.2, that is the idea of The Asset Partnership pursuing a public training course venture, we have simply shown the risk analysis which was conducted on this one idea. This was one idea which came out of an overall strategic review which was carried out using a SWOT analysis. There were many other ideas raised in the opportunities part of this SWOT analysis and as part of a brainstorming exercise. For each of these ideas a risk analysis was conducted in the same way as that described. It can be seen from this that risk analysis can be a time-consuming activity if carried out properly. If, however, you are working through this sort of major exercise with a team you can split the group into subgroups. Each subgroup then works on just a few of the ideas and then presents their risk analysis to the rest of the group. Working in parallel in this way can save a lot of time in the overall exercise.

THE CASE FOR CONTINGENCY PLANNING

The contingency planning stage of the risk analysis process is where contingent measures are decided which will actually be built into the planning and implementation stages. We contingency plan where it has been decided that it is still worthwhile pursuing a course of action so long as the serious risks are managed.

This point is probably best illustrated by building on our working case study. We decided that given the risks associated with the public training course strategy it was still worth pursuing the idea into implementation. We were conscious though of the need to manage the high risk factors and therefore we drew up formal contingency plans around the four highest risks identified. This contingency planning is shown in Figure 6.3.

As a result of the risk analysis it is possible to identify which risks should be managed if proceeding with an activity. It also may be considered appropriate to reassess whether to proceed with a course of action. Ultimately, then, a number of decisions will now be processed on to the detailed planning, implementation and action planning stages. In the next chapter we will consider a number of techniques for action planning, monitoring and control as the final stage in the ADAPT model.

Risk	Contingency plan
Risk also of database becoming out of date	Plan to 'future proof' the database by building in ongoing updating facility. Make resources available for checking on key people on database to ensure that details on people changing jobs are incorporated
Do not have sufficient to run major technology database	Conduct technical research and costings analysis to identify suitable technical strategy. Consider purchase/hire/ subcontracting options
Having to front-end load funding of such a project — could run out of funds unless generate sufficient delegates to make the project pay	Ensure that initial courses are well supported by offering special rates for existing clients to ensure breakeven figure reached Subsidise the project from income from other parts of the business in the first six months then ensure project is self-funding
Could get pricing of courses wrong and fail to attract interest	Conduct competitor analysis and discuss proposed pricing structure with clients

Figure 6.3 *Contingency planning*

PAUSE FOR THOUGHT

■ *Consider a particular action you as an individual or as part of a group or team are about to take*

■ *Using this real example of an intended action conduct a risk analysis*

■ *What are the various risks?*

■ *Weight the probability of each risk materialising (0–1)*

■ *Weight the potential impact if the risk does materialise (0–10)*

■ *Multiple the probability and the impact figure in order to produce an overall picture of the relative value of the different risks*

■ *Consider how you could actually manage the highest of these risks by putting contingency plans in place.*

7

PRACTICAL PLANNING

'It's a bad plan that admits of no modification.'

Publilius Syrus

In 'Practical Planning' we will:

■ *Build on our understanding of risk analysis and how it links with the planning and control process*
■ *Consider methods of prioritising where to start when planning broad projects which entail several actions to be implemented over a period of time*
■ *Suggest a simple framework for identifying key account-abilities in the implementation of a project through tactical planning*
■ *Discuss specific planning tools and techniques, including approaches to backward planning, Network Planning and the use of Gantt Charts*
■ *Explain how to establish individual targets as an aid to planning and control.*

Planning and control are two highly integrated activities; when effective the planning and control process ensure that projects continuously improve and develop. It is recognised that with the increasing rate of change facing many organisations, it is no longer possible simply to analyse a problem, formulate decisions, implement them and then wait for the correct results. In particular with open or more strategic problems there will be a number of variables which are difficult to predict in an absolute sense at the planning stage. While contingency planning as a result of risk analysis will help us to anticipate and reduce the negative impact of potential problems it is likely in reality that, due to the dynamic nature of project management, there will be factors and issues which arise during implementation which need to be addressed. This clearly calls for both flexibility in being able to modify and adjust plans as a result of the monitoring process.

Here we will first of all consider some basic approaches to planning, starting with providing an overview of the business planning process which was first mentioned in chapter one.

Planning is primarily concerned with implementing solutions to problems and means developing specific action plans. Often it is difficult when planning on a broad scale to decide where to start and we will provide a framework which helps you to prioritise which issues to commence with and then how to proceed with implementation.

There are many ways in which you can provide an overview of the plan and the main criteria in selecting an approach to planning should be that you are able to identify who is responsible for achieving what and by when. As long as these issues are agreed then the process of monitoring progress and identifying whether the plans are progressing or slipping becomes much more easy. With more complex projects there may be a need for a more sophisticated approach to planning and here we will look at the value to be gained from using some of the classic project planning and monitoring tools such as Network Planning and Gantt Charts.

Control is about measuring progress and providing feedback. This often results in the problem being defined and analysed further resulting in further decision making; in other words we work through the steps of the ADAPT model again but with more advanced information. This suggests that the model might be viewed more as a continuous cycle than as simply a process with a beginning and ending. Figure 7.1 shows the process of planning, implementation and control as a continuous cycle.

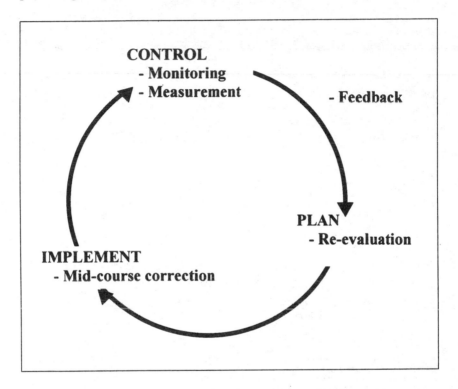

Figure 7.1 *Cycle of planning and control*

CHARACTERISTICS OF PLANNING

Despite the fact that many planning techniques would appear to be quite detailed and elaborate it should be emphasised that the process of planning is really far from a precise science. However if plans are made with due consideration of key issues such as the resources available, the parameters or constraints, and if a structured approach has been taken to the prior stages of problem solving as described in the previous chapters, then it is more likely that plans will be realistic and therefore the process of monitoring and control will become easier.

All planning requires us to make some assumptions and forecasts and this is considered quite legitimate, though where this is the case they should be stated explicitly. Forecasts themselves are about measuring or assessing uncertainty and they should be treated as useful rather than precise. The plan should point the way forward in as specific a way as is possible at the time the plan is produced. Naturally the plan will need to be revisited on a regular basis and adjusted accordingly.

In order to understand the skills of effective planning it is worthwhile reflecting on the context and nature of the overall planning process.

1. Planning is future-focused and as such there is always an element of unpredictability when plans are made, however planning requires decision making in the present as well as in the future
2. Planning seeks to change or anticipate and responds to environmental changes when they occur
3. All planning involves the use of forecasts and assumptions; also inherent in the planning process are our own values and beliefs
4. It must be viewed as a dynamic process that does not necessarily have a beginning and an end. However, plans should be formalised in writing
5. Plans should always be centred around the organisational, team or project mission or vision, as well as specific business objectives
6. Planning often involves a trade-off between organisational objectives and personal goals.

In a business problem-solving situation, or when we are involved in project planning it is necessary to recognise that planning takes place at several different levels. These might be described as:

▓ Strategic
▓ Operational.

Strategic plans tend to take a 'big picture' approach and look at what needs to be achieved often under broad strategic headings. So an organisation may have a strategic business plan, a strategic plan for developing people or a strategic plan with respect to technology. Whatever the subject matter of the strategic plan it will tend to address broad issues which will help in achieving movement towards the overall vision. Strategic plans are often long term, covering a period of, say, one to five years.

Whereas the strategic plan identifies what is to be achieved the operational or tactical plan looks at how the plan is to be achieved. Execution of the operational plan will contribute towards the achievement of the strategic plan. At this level planning will tend to identify specific issues such as who is going to do what and by when.

While it is of course advantageous for all parties involved in a project to have sight of all the plans, those at the operational level who are involved with implementation will tend to work from the operational plan.

Interestingly we believe that a different skill set is required by those who are working on strategic planning compared to those working with operational plans. For strategic planning it is important to be able to step back from the immediate day-to-day environment and to see things in their historical context. Equally, there is a need to be able to postulate as to how things might be in the future. Some people are clearly more comfortable than others at looking ahead in this way. Strategic planning also requires an awareness of issues outside the immediate project or organisational environment. So in business strategic planning it is essential to be aware of those factors which might impinge on the plans once you have moved into the implementation stage. This might include for instance economic or political factors or the approaches being taken by the competition. Strategic planning considerations may include issues of economy, suppliers, technology, competitors, customers, socio-political factors and issues of government.

For those involved with operational planning there is a need to be able to deal with detail and to consider specific issues such as who should be involved and in what way. There will be a need for awareness of internal factors such as finance, management, employees, capital equipment, research and development, products and services.

There are many reasons why planning fails and we have listed below some of the most common:

▦ Lack of overall vision/goals
▦ Estimates are based on best guesses rather than standards or empirical data
▦ Assumptions are not recognised
▦ Plans encompass too much, or too little time
▦ Poor quality of data
▦ Lack of clear milestones
▦ Lack of a systematic process
▦ Poor level of earlier analysis
▦ Based on poor financial estimates.

Finally it has been our experience to note that many plans fail when the responsibility for the planning process is given just to one individual or group. We believe that planning should be both vertical and horizontal involving many people. By involving many representatives in the planning process it is more likely that a number of perspectives will be incorporated rather than the views or opinions of just one person or group as to how things should be done. Additionally the advantage of involving several parties is that the process of implementation is likely to be easier and more realistic. If people have been involved in the planning process then they are more likely to buy into implementation rather than having to implement plans which have been foisted on them by others.

PRIORITISATION FOR PLANNING

If you have been working on a major open or strategic problem then it may be the case that when you come to the planning stage you have so many plans to implement that you are unsure of exactly where to start. If this is the case you need some structured way of deciding which plans need to be implemented before others. One useful tool here is the use of the Speed Versus Impact method of prioritisation. This is shown in Figure 7.2.

As can be seen from Figure 7.2 this approach to prioritisation works on the basis that we can make a judgement about each

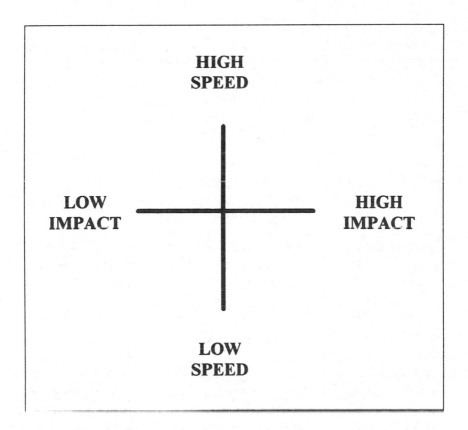

Figure 7.2 *Speed versus impact method of prioritisation*

proposed plan with regard to its impact and the speed at which it can be implemented. If for instance as part of a major problem-solving exercise you have identified 40 things which you want to do and you now need to decide where to start in terms of detailed planning and then implementation you would apply the techniques in the following way.

▨   First list the 40 items
▨   Next number these items 1–40
▨   Now plot these items by their number on the chart as shown in Figure 7.2. They will be plotted in a position on the chart based on a judgement which is made by those in the planning group about their relative impact and speed of implementation.

Impact refers to the extent to which successful implementation of the plan will make an impact on the overall business of achievement of the overall goal or vision. *Speed* refers to how quickly it will be possible to implement the plan. Some plans can be implemented relatively speedily because there are less political or cost constraints for example.

Having plotted the 40 plans on the chart you are now in a position to decide where to start and logically you should start by implementing those plans which fall into the top right quadrant (high speed, high impact).

Beyond this you will need to make a decision as to which quadrant you tackle as second, third and fourth priorities and this will vary depending on the nature of the project.

TACTICAL PLANNING

Wherever possible planning should be kept as simple as possible, though as we will see when we look at the techniques for planning major projects, this is often easier said than done. If however you are able to break the plans down into discrete areas or packages it can be helpful to use the approach suggested in Figure 7.3. Here we see how a tactical plan might be drawn up to cover specifics such as who is to do what and why and what are the expected time-scales. The advantage of this approach to tactical planning is that if several of these plans have to be drawn up and if you are working in a project or team, then such tactical planning can be carried out by subgroups and these can be selected on the basis of who is able to contribute effectively to planning against different topics. Such tactical plans can then be distributed once they have been agreed and relevant parties are left in no doubt as to where the responsibility for action actually lies.

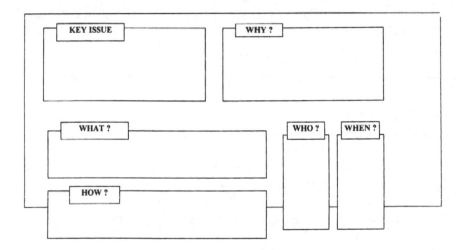

Figure 7.3 *Tactical action plans*

PROJECT PLANNING AND CONTROL

In dealing with smaller projects which involve only one or two parties and where it is relatively easy to identify all the relevant actions to be taken it may be easy enough to use a traditional approach to planning activities by starting at the beginning and then planning forwards. So for instance if you are planning to run a meeting in order to review customer orders the simple plan might look like this:

1. Decide on attendees
2. Agree agenda with attendees
3. Fix date and time
4. Arrange location
5. Pre meeting research
6. Organise roles in meeting (chairperson, minute taker, time-keeper)
7. Run meeting
8. Review.

For larger projects though the process of planning might not be quite so simple and it may be helpful to consider what we refer to as backward planning. With backward planning you start by asking questions regarding the end result which is expected.

So for example a project might be to introduce a new product to the marketplace. First the ultimate outcome is defined:

■ To deliver a product to market by December which broadens our product portfolio and meets a real need.

Next we ask what must be done immediately prior to this being achieved. The answer could be:

■ The product must be launched with appropriate advertising.

The same approach is continued by asking 'What must precede this activity?'. This backward plan might 'precede' as follows:

■ Advertising media to be selected
■ Type of advertisements and publicity to be decided
■ Final product design to be agreed
■ Packaging and colours to be selected
■ Final design of actual product to be agreed
■ Test marketing of various designs
■ Initial design work to be done
■ Designers to be briefed
■ Product positioning in existing portfolio to be agreed.

The advantage of backward planning is that it starts with the end in mind; consideration is given right at the start as to what the customer or client, whether internal or external, actually wants. It also helps to ensure that those areas which are important in the later phases of the project, which might otherwise be forgotten, are actually considered.

When the project is substantial and involves a number of different parties it is often necessary to recognise that some activities are dependent on others and some are independent. In this case you might consider the use of Network Planning. The network shows the preferable order in which activities should be completed, which tasks have to be completed sequentially and which ones can be completed in parallel.

In the example of a Network Plan shown (Figure 7.4) you can see that we have identified the key tasks which need to be achieved in working towards the achievement of a particular goal in our own business. In this example the goal is successfully to market and launch a public training course. Incidentally this was just one of the goals which fitted into our overall marketing strategy. It was recognised though that this was a new venture and entailed some critical planning if we were to meet our own deadlines for completion.

Having identified the various tasks which were to be achieved it can be seen that we firstly listed them and allocated a number to them. Then working from left to right we plotted which activities were dependent on which others. It can be seen that some items are dependent on just one other activity, eg activity 7 (developing the course training materials) is dependent on activity 6 (short lead purchases which includes purchase of files, folders, stationery etc).

Some items are seen to have a multiple dependency, for example activity 4 (development and design of the course) must be completed before activity 5 (identifying resources for the course) and activity 8 (reproduction of materials for the course) can be completed. It is also possible in some cases for more than one activity to be progressed at the same time. So for

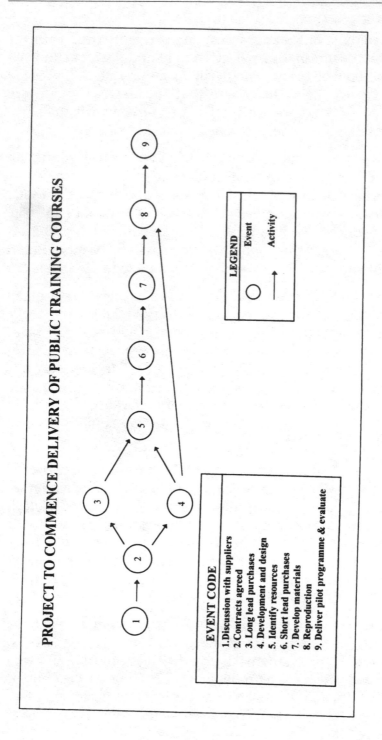

PROJECT TO COMMENCE DELIVERY OF PUBLIC TRAINING COURSES

EVENT CODE

1. Discussion with suppliers
2. Contracts agreed
3. Long lead purchases
4. Development and design
5. Identify resources
6. Short lead purchases
7. Develop materials
8. Reproduction
9. Deliver pilot programme & evaluate

LEGEND

◯ Event

→ Activity

Figure 7.4 *Worked example of a Network Plan*

instance activity 3 (long lead purchases of, for instance audio visual equipment) and activity 4 (development and design of the materials) can be covered at the same time but both must be completed before activity 5 can commence.

So in producing a Network Plan such as this you should be asking questions such as:

▨ What activities must be completed before another one can commence?
▨ What can be done at the same time?
▨ What activities cannot commence until another one is complete?

If the activities are many, varied and complex it may be necessary to estimate the time required for completion of each task and these can be added into the diagram as appropriate. Normally you will be able to estimate these through a process of discussion though there are more involved ways of trying to estimate duration.

An advanced approach is to identify the critical path; this is the path showing those activities which are critical to the project progressing. This is often referred to as a Critical Path Analysis.

Step description	Done by	Responsible	Time (weeks)
1. Discussion with suppliers	Madeleine	David	2
2. Contracts agreed	Peter	Peter	1
3. Long lead purchases	David	Richard	5
4. Development and design	Richard	Peter	2
5. Identify resources	David	David	2
6. Short lead purchases	Madeleine	Peter	3
7. Develop materials	Sharon	Peter	3
8. Reproduction	Shan	Richard	2
9. Deliver pilot and evaluate	Peter/Richard	Peter/Richard	2

Figure 7.5 *Identifying the Critical Path*

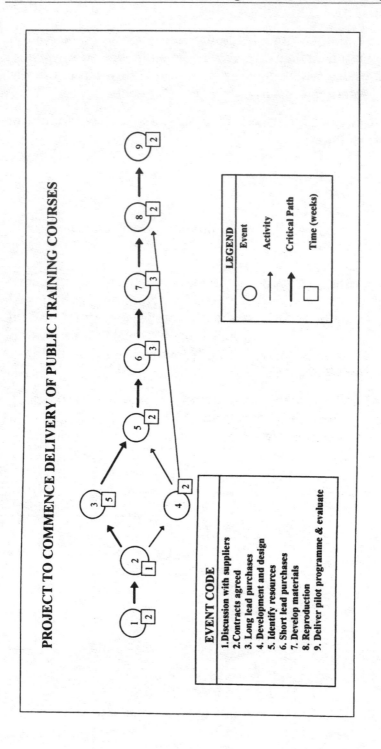

Figure 7.6 *Identifying the critical path on the Network Plan*

In this example in Figure 7.5 we have differentiated between who will be involved in actually doing certain tasks and who has the overall responsibility for them. We have identified the time to be allowed for each task and now can plot this on to the Network Plan as shown in Figure 7.6.

Having now identified and plotted the estimated time for each activity the next stage is to identify the critical path. This is calculated by adding the times along each chain of arrows from the start to the end of the diagram. The path with the largest total time is referred to as the critical path and the activities along this path are considered critical because they control the duration of the project as a whole. In implementing and monitoring the plans particular attention should be paid to ensuring these activities are completed on time otherwise the whole project time-scale will slip.

So to summarise, this approach to project planning shows all the activities and their inter-relationships in the form of a network. By considering the time and resources needed to complete each of these activities it is possible to locate the critical path of activities. This path is the sequence of activities and events whose accomplishments will require the greatest expected time.

The Network Plan also enables us to examine the impact changes in one activity of a project has on others and so track the implications of deviations from the plan.

The technique of Critical Path Analysis is particularly appropriate in projects where there is a definitive start and finish date, for example in developing new services or, as our worked example shows, when launching a new product.

Network Planning enables us to split the project up into smaller parts and by estimating duration it provides greater accuracy and allows the consequences of changes in plans to be considered before implementing those changes.

In addition to Network Planning as described above another commonly used and useful planning tool is the Gantt Chart. The

Gantt Chart is named after the American engineer Henry Gantt who developed this technique as a way of depicting the progress of projects in relation to time. In general terms this approach is suitable for less complex tasks, but the following points should be considered:

■ Gantt Charts are only really applicable where time estimates are very accurate and are unlikely to change
■ Large projects are made up of many interrelated tasks and these cannot usually be shown effectively
■ Interdependencies cannot be depicted
■ They do not allow for resource allocation against activities nor for cost control.

Examples: a simple Gantt Chart is shown in Figure 7.7. This approach identifies the activities to be completed and lists these, then plots across the page the time period when activities should commence and when they should complete. This does provide a good overview of how activities may overlap and can help with scheduling and overall planning. Additionally, as shown in the example, it is possible to plot activities which have been completed as and when they are achieved.

So we have shown in this chapter a number of approaches to project planning and it can be seen that these techniques tend also to inform the process of monitoring, reviewing and therefore controlling activities. Where the problem-solving process is much more tactical (probably in 80 per cent of cases) then we recommend a simple tactical action-planning process which shows the issue, why it is an issue, and who does what and how and by when. With more complex projects then more advanced planning and monitoring systems will need to be established as described above.

SETTING TARGETS AND OBJECTIVES

Having undertaken the basic process of planning, next it is important to consider what resources are required and when

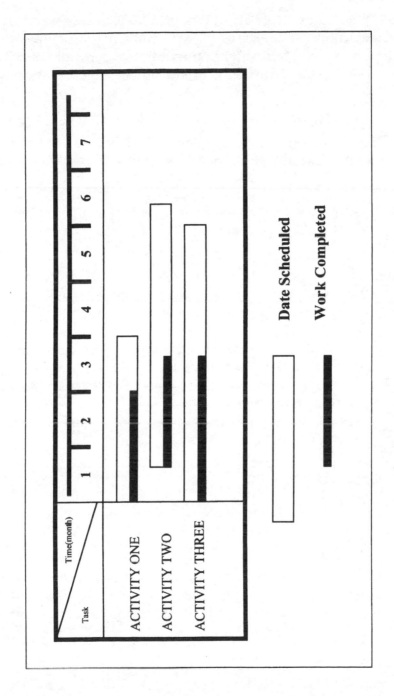

Figure 7.7 *Planning with Gantt Charts*

these will be needed. As part of this process it is necessary to determine who will be responsible for completing which parts of the plan. Specific objectives should be set for individuals and here we consider the issue of individual target setting in more depth.

In many organisations the process of target setting is tackled as part of the performance appraisal and review system and while this makes a lot of sense you do not have to have an appraisal scheme in order to establish individual targets. Arguably in any project, while the group or team as a whole will be responsible for producing results and implementing plans, there is a need to identify specifically what is expected of individuals.

Different organisations and indeed different levels of staff within an organisation will use different terms to describe targets. Very often words like goals, targets or objectives are used.

- An organisation may set a strategic objective to command 20 per cent of market share in its industry...
- A function may set an objective to meet the organisation's manufacturing requirements...
- A team objective might be to complete a particular project on time within budget and to a specification.

Such objectives, to be useful should be specific enough to provide something to aim at which can be measured and evaluated in terms of success. Additionally such objectives should fit in with the organisation's or project's overall strategic goals and overall vision.

The process of turning organisational and departmental objectives into individual performance targets will be influenced both by the organisation's approach to objective setting and the style of individual managers.

Performance objectives can be used for a range of purposes:

- They may be the vehicle for implementation of the organisation's policy and strategy
- They may form the basis for managing and monitoring individual performance and contribution towards the bigger plan
- They may help individuals or teams to plan their own work.

Performance objectives may be set in terms of output. Typically output-related objectives will stress the amount of performance required; for example a sales representative may be expected to make so many sales per week while an assembly worker may be expected to produce so many items per day. Such objectives should fit in with the broader plan.

At this stage it is appropriate to spend some time considering the issue of personal targets which focus on behaviours. The subject of how to define competences associated with human behaviour is far from easy. To understand this important theme, see the model shown in Figure 7.8.

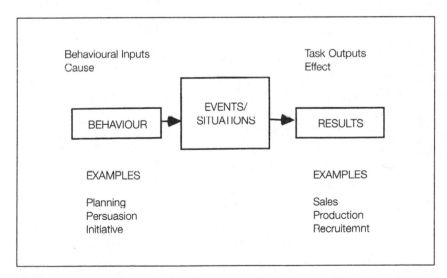

Source: Hale, R I and Whitlam, P J (1995) *Target Setting and Goal Achievement,* Kogan Page, London

Figure 7.8 *Behavioural inputs and task outputs*

This model shows that any outputs which an individual might achieve are actually the result of that person displaying certain behaviours, which might be described as inputs. If targets or objectives focus exclusively on the achievement of task outputs then there can be problems such as the employee not understanding how to go about achieving results or, even more damaging potentially, there is the danger of achieving results against the target but causing more disruption in the process than is often realised.

With the growth in interest in target setting there has been an overemphasis on setting output-related targets, so for example individuals have to:

◼ Increase sales by x per cent
◼ Decrease complaints by y per cent
◼ Increase the production rate by z per cent

It has been shown that there are some significant benefits to be gained from personal target setting if it is handled appropriately. In particular it has been shown that:

◼ Production increases in organisations which set goals or targets for individuals effectively
◼ Effective target setting in performance review serves as a motivational force
◼ There is a tendency to show leniency in performance evaluation which can be countered if goals or targets are set effectively in specific terms.

It is important to be able to define what successful performance looks like and to that end one should seek to include success criteria in setting targets. Success criteria might be based around, for instance:

◼ Cost — performing a task within certain cost perameters
◼ Speed — being able to do a task at a certain speed
◼ Deadlines — meeting a deadline which is set

■ Accuracy — being able to work to a certain level of accuracy
■ Skills — able to demonstrate new levels of skill
■ Level of supervision — able to operate without supervision.

The key is for the manager to be able to judge the level of performance which is appropriate for the individual concerned. A useful framework for target setting is to ensure that targets are SMART:

■ **Specific** — enough to have meaning rather than being expressed in generalities
■ **Measurable** — including measure of success and expected performance
■ **Acceptable** — as a result of two-way discussion at the formulation stage
■ **Realistic** — but providing sufficient challenge to stretch the individual
■ **Timebound** — with some deadline or guidance on timing for achievement.

It has been increasingly recognised that in managing the performance of others, target setting should be seen as a two-way process whereby the individual makes a commitment to work towards the achievement of a target and the manager makes a commitment to the individual to help him or her to achieve the targets. Certainly the individual is likely to be more motivated in working towards the targets if assistance and co-operation is available from the manager.

So in the last section of this chapter we have discussed some of the key issues to be aware of in translating the broader organisational issues of project plans into individual targets or objectives. The important point is to ensure that a structured approach is taken to identifying just what has to be done and by whom. By taking as specific an approach as possible the whole area of monitoring and control of the project becomes more easy.

PAUSE FOR THOUGHT

■ *Identify a project on which you are working or are about to work on.*

■ *Using one of the approaches to planning defined in this chapter, formulate a plan for this project. Approaches discussed were:*
— *Backward planning*
— *Network Planning*
— *Gantt Charts.*

■ *Set a developmental target for yourself, your boss or your subordinate which adheres to the principles of effective target or objective setting as described above and contributes to a broader plan.*

■ *Ensure that your target adheres to the principles of SMART targets as defined above.*

CONCLUDING OVERVIEW

In this 'Concluding Overview' we:

- *Provide a brief overview of the main messages of the book*
- *Present an overall picture of the ADAPT model showing how the key stages are related, and some of the techniques which might be used as you work through the model.*

OVERVIEW OF MATERIAL

At this stage it is considered useful to provide a brief overview of the main messages from the preceding chapters. This is meant as an overall summary and will help you to consider the key stages in the ADAPT model and the main arguments for taking a structured approach to problem solving and decision making.

We started the book by looking at the reason why taking a structured approach to problem solving and decision making is becoming increasingly important. There are clearly a number of external factors and forces. For instance people are increasingly having to seek approval from others or persuade them to do things and in doing so are likely to be more successful if able to demonstrate how a particular decision or proposal has been arrived at.

Equally the sheer rate of change which we are having to cope with means that there are certain seemingly opposed determining forces; on the one hand we have too little information and on the other we are suffering from information overload. This suggests a real need either to create data or to make realistic assumptions where there are no obvious answers, and to manage the data we do have effectively. There is no doubt that the quality of decisions made will be determined by the effectiveness with which data is managed.

We suggested that in considering the nature of problems, broadly speaking it is possible to consider that some problems are more open and others are more closed. With open problems there may be several answers, there will be no one recognised way of solving the problem and the problem may well be related to other broader problems. Generally speaking most strategic issues present as open problems. In addressing open problems we suggest using certain techniques which help first to explore and understand the problem in some depth before seeking solutions. A useful approach particularly when working with groups is to start by defining the objectives of the group through the development of some sort of vision statement; the process of developing a vision, while challenging, serves to unite the group behind a common picture of success.

We explored a number of the classic barriers to problem solving which actually make it difficult and showed how many of these are related to human behaviour and differences. Frequently we do not really know where to start in tackling a problem; it just seems too big or complex and it may be appropriate to develop a Problem Specification showing both what the problem is and what it is not. It may be helpful to use the Seven Ms framework at this stage, as indeed at many other stages in the process of problem solving. Usually we approach a problem on an individual basis from our own very unique perspective and it is easy to lose sight of the fact that other people have other and different perspectives; here the Perspective Specification can help in considering matters from different perspectives and in anticipating the views or arguments which other parties might present.

In presenting the overall picture of the ADAPT (Analysis, Decision Making, Active Risk Taking, Planning and Transition) model, we believe that while the component parts of this model are not necessarily unique or totally original, what we do provide which is original is a structured way of showing how these stages in problem solving and the associated techniques actually fit together. These key stages are as follows.

First, problem formulation whereby a better understanding of the problem is developed and where a vision of success is agreed. Next is the major stage in terms of time allocation which is about producing ideas to solve the problem through analysis. Here a number of analytical techniques might be used, the SWOT analysis being by far the most widely used strategic analysis technique. The idea of the analysis stage is to generate a high volume of ideas which can then be considered further at the decision-making stage. We also discussed under the analysis stage techniques such as the Fishbone Analysis and the Why, Why Analysis which were more appropriate for the more closed problems.

The stage of decision making is divided clearly into three distinct steps. First the Decision-making Framework is drawn up; here the key criteria are defined. This is in effect the reality check and will often entail the identification of financial and other resource constraints.

Recognising that until now in the model the emphasis has been placed on logical and systematic thinking, the next step in the decision-making stage is to develop alternatives. There is a need to harness creative energy through creative techniques such as brainstorming which is a way of developing alternative ideas. In this way we can be assured that the options for tackling the problem have been addressed most thoroughly. All of the potential ideas are then filtered through the Decision-making Framework as the third part of the decision-making step. In this way the high volume of ideas is reduced to a realistic number.

Taking those ideas which pass through this filter, the next major step is risk analysis. Here potential risks in taking a given course of action are identified and these are then weighted accordingly. This provides the information which is required in deciding whether to proceed with a course of action or if proceeding, how to manage the most significant risks.

This then leads directly into the planning stage and we looked at a number of approaches to planning, monitoring and controlling, including the major project monitoring technique, Network Analysis. If you have been involved in a major strategic level problem-solving exercise it may well be the case that you still have a high number of possible actions to take having reached the planning stage; in this case it may be helpful to prioritise plans based on how quickly they can be implemented and what level of impact they are likely to have.

The key stages in the ADAPT model and associated techniques are shown for the sake of summary in Figure 8.1.

While we have presented what is a highly structured model to use in approaching problems, this should not restrict you in deciding which technique to use at the appropriate time. The key point is that you should choose the most relevant tool or technique for the circumstances. We accept that there will be many more techniques than those which we have presented. Nonetheless before using any technique you should consider questions such as 'What are we seeking to get out of this?', 'Are we seeking to be creative or analytical here?' and 'Does everyone in the group know how to use the technique?'

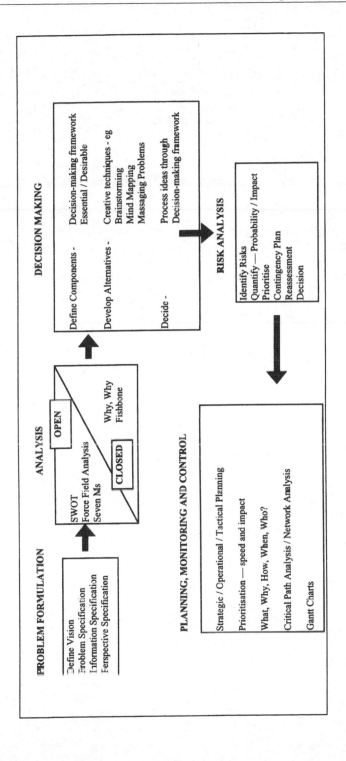

Figure 8.1 *Key stages and techniques in the ADAPT model of problem solving and decision making*

SELECTED READING LIST

Bird, M (1993) *Problem Solving Techniques That Really Work*, Piatkus, London

Buzan, T (1989) *Use Your Head,* BBC, London

Hale, R I and Whitlam, P J (1995) *The Power of Personal Influence*, McGraw-Hill, Maidenhead

Hale, R I and Whitlam, P J (1995) *Target Setting and Goal Achievement*, Kogan Page, London

Hale, R I and Whitlam, P J (1997) *Towards the Virtual Organisation*, McGraw-Hill, Maidenhead

Kelly, P (1995) *Team Decision Making Techniques*, Kogan Page, London

Kirkton, M (1989) *Adaptors and Innovators: Styles of Creativity and Problem Solving*, Routledge, London

Leigh, A (1988) *Effective Change*, IPM, London

Locke, E and Latham, G (1990) *A Theory Of Goal Setting*, Prentice-Hall, New York

Parker, G (1995) *Structured Problem Solving*, Gower, Aldershot

Pokras, S (1990) *Systematic Problem Solving and Decision Making*, Kogan Page, London

Rickards, T (1990) *Creativity and Problem Solving at Work*, Gower, Aldershot

The authors would be pleased to hear from you if you would like to discuss this publication further or explore opportunities for running training courses or seminars. Please contact:

Dr. Peter Whitlam
Mr. Richard Hale
The Asset Partnership
Broom Hill
21 Cliff Drive
Cromer
Norfolk NR27 0AW
United Kingdom

Tel/fax: +44 1263 515150
e-mail: whitlam@asset.co.uk
        rhale@asset.co.uk

INDEX